Another Level

How Changing Your Mindset Changes Your Circumstances

Ms. Twanja Windley

Don't ever dismiss someone's thoughts until you can see things from their point of view.

Table of Contents

Introduction

The purpose of this book is to help people find healing from the scars of life. It is to show them that everyone has scars, although some are less visible, hidden behind shame, guilt, and sometimes even a smile. Sometimes, we can get stuck in situations without knowing how to move forward. We can become so ashamed that we apply a coating of false perfection to make people believe we are living our best lives while we fraud our way through. There are also people who are stuck because they aren't able to see past their current situations; I used to feel that way.

Life would knock me down, and instead of healing, I kept looking at my scars as a reminder of what I had been through. Shamefully, I would cover it up and pretend that I was ok, but deep down inside, I had reached my breaking point. Like Humpty Dumpy, the day came when I fell off the wall. You see, the wall was the only thing holding me up. I knew that someday I would shatter, but I didn't want people to see me break. I also feared what others would think about me. I preferred to hide and sweep things under the rug rather than to heal and fix the things that had been chipping away at me for years. You can never heal from the pain when you keep going back to look at it. Instead of using it as a stepping stone, I used it as a reminder of how badly life treated me. I kept going back to feel that pain, wondering if I touched it, would it still be there. Even when the pain dissipated and I felt I had healed enough, I would revisit that place, only to realize I wasn't healed at all. My constant "need" to revisit that place stopped my ability to fully heal from it, but you can never heal from pain when you keep going back to revisit it.

Think about the person who struggled with losing weight. That person looked in the mirror everyday staring at their body feeling like they couldn't do anything about it. I was once that person too. Instead of telling myself, "I can do this," I would convince myself that I would start the next day or the day after that. Before I knew it, a year had gone by and I was still trying to get started. That's life and so many people go through that phase. I used to think I had to be in a certain place for God to reach me. We often feel like we need to be in a certain place in life for things to change, but the truth is I could stand in that very moment, and just like Blind Bartimaeus, call the name of Jesus. God would have come to me like he did the town sinner with no judgement. He would have seen my heart and my desire. I detached from God because of all of my mistakes but believing in that was a falsehood. I finally realized I didn't have to wait until my life was "good enough" to seek God. I could find him in that exact moment with all of my flaws, naked and unashamed, carrying all my extra weight. There was nothing to hide because He knew me and knew my story before I started to live it.

Think about that for a moment. I know it sounds surreal, but it's true. God knew my story, my journey, what would come before I even took my first breath. All the blessings in my life were willed by Him. He loves me so much that he blessed me before I got here. God loves us all and will give you the strength to conquer anything you set out to do. There are no limitations to what God can do and there is no time frame to get started.

If there was one thing that I want you to get from this book, it is to recognize that we are all human and we all experience the same things, no matter how life attacks, no matter who you really are under your makeup. I want you to understand that the pain you are going through; you are not alone. We may see people and think they have life figured out, but the truth is we are in this fight together. If you keep reading, you will see that I'm fighting with you. Everything that we go through is necessary because purpose is birthed out of pain.

I had to learn this for myself. There have been times when I reflected on my past and regretted some of the choices that I've made. However, when I look at the place from which God has brought me, I am thankful for the mistakes that allowed God to redirect my path, to change my outlook and my thought process. Making mistakes provides learning experiences. Even though I have some regrets about the path that I have chosen, if I continue to keep moving forward, my dreams are going to happen. We must trust the process in all that we do. It won't happen overnight, but it won't ever happen if we quit. The only guarantee for failure is quitting!

My desire is to inspire people and to give hope when it feels like all hope is lost. I remember going out daily, hoping to receive a word from God. I just wanted to hear something comforting. I thought maybe God would send someone to speak something encouraging into my life or tell me what my future would look like. I was desperate for direction. The truth is, I already had everything I needed to live a life of true fulfillment. Everything I needed for my destiny was within reach. I had been carrying my future inside of me this whole time. I just needed to get it out and every promise was written.

As I embarked on this journey, I found things inside of me that I never knew existed. I discovered more about myself, about the person that I was called to be, and what was inside of me all along. Never beat yourself up if life knocks you down, get back up and keep trying.

I believe that this book can become a reference for you to utilize when you feel like you need to shift your mindset. These insights could guide you in changing your thought process, which can make a difference in your life. The more I sought God's wisdom, the closer I felt to him. I woke up everyday wanting to be closer to Him. My circumstances taught me to love myself, and I believe that past obstacles against me have allowed me to grow. Everything in life has a process that must take its course. In life, we go from phase to phase, level to level, and greater to greater. Life isn't an easy journey, but when we hold onto the promises that God has given us, it becomes our weapon to speak life over our situation.

Prologue:
The Push

Are you rising above your storm? It's time to push yourself into purpose. You can push your vision to a place you have never imagined. You can push yourself to the next level of your journey. As you commit to pushing yourself, ask if you are willing to commit your life to do what God has called you to do?

The Bible teaches us, "They who wait on the Lord shall renew their strength; they shall mount up with wings like eagles; they shall run, and not be weary; they shall walk and not faint" (Isaiah 40:31). When the uneasiness of life disrupts us, it doesn't have to win. Do you know what an eagle does when a storm is coming? The eagle will fly to a high spot and wait for the winds to arrive. When the storm hits, the eagle will move its wings so the wind can pick it up and lift it above the storm. While the storm rages below, the eagle soars above. When the storm of life comes upon us, we must rise above it just like the eagle and allow it to lift us higher. Let the winds that bring turmoil into our lives elevate us to the next level so that we can overcome the storm.

Through my struggles, I've learned that my circumstances don't dictate my happiness. Even at my lowest points, when I didn't think I could make it, life has taught me that when I remain in control of my own thoughts, I control the direction I wanted to head into. My main focus is to keep my head in the game because whatever I allow to dominate my thought process has control over me. When I give special attention to anything, it will grow and magnify in my life. These words are a caution to heed the direction your thoughts take you because they control your mind. I control the size of something by how I process it in my mind. It's not always easy.

There were days when I felt like giving up and throwing in the towel. It was a time when life was winning, and I was being dragged by it. There were mornings when I didn't want to get out of my car and head into work, days when I didn't want to get out of bed and face life. There were nights when I didn't even want to go home and face the people who were counting on me. I tried avoiding everything – took no phone calls, didn't see my family or friends, didn't attend any events. I just wanted to suffer alone. I was sulking and wanted to stay in that miserable place. I wasn't ready to move from it. I wanted to feel the pain and rehearse those bad memories. I couldn't fight back. Maybe I didn't have the strength to fight. I was stuck!

There were prayers and no answers, seeds but no harvest, praise and no breakthrough. I cried out, "Where are you, God?!" Suddenly, something turned for me. It turned in a way that brought me joy. Maybe it was because I was still praying even though I didn't want to, or maybe it was just time to move forward. Something different started happening within me. I was pressing into God in a way that I had never done before. I started winning from within. The words I had spoken over my life started to work within me and I came to realize that my life wasn't what it appeared to be.

Have you ever taken a prescription and needed to give it time to start working on a symptom or sickness within you? That is exactly what this change felt like. I was meditating on God's words, but I had to give them time to start working within me. A doctor would recommend that you use that prescription for the duration of time he suggests. So, why would we stop seeking God once we begin to feel a slight bit of relief? Just like the prescribed medication once we feel somewhat alleviated from our symptoms, we reduced the level of strength we once applied because we no longer need Him in the same capacity as we started with. Why can't we yield into God, so that we can fight off what is trying to take hold of us?

Once my spirit lifted, I found a new tune to sing and I got my joy back. I got my peace back. I took it back. I started fighting for a clear mind and mental peace. I had to close the door on the people and things that were in my path and not a part of my journey to maintain peace. Peace is what I look forward to daily. I want to encourage you to find peace in every situation. Peace is from within us and if you lose your peace, that means you have given it away. I had to remind myself that no one could take anything away from me if I didn't allow them to. Peace belongs to me.

During my college days, my roommates wanted to go out to the club. I wasn't the partying type, but I would always go because that is what everyone else was doing.

"Come on, you are always in the house and never do anything," my roommates would say. When I did go out, it would be with my family or the friends I grew up with. I knew I could hold them accountable if something would happen.

One night, Pastor Troy, the rapper, was at this particular club and it was twenty dollars to get in. I had already heard Pastor Troy in concert many times, so I had no desire to see him in concert again. I also had no desire to give up my last twenty dollars just to be thrown out of the club because I could guarantee a fight would break out.

When we arrived, the line was long like it was for Black Friday specials. We were freezing our behinds off in the cold, waiting to get into this club. I silently prayed that we wouldn't be able to get in the club. Have you ever done something because someone else wanted you to, deep inside you were against it, but were just following the crowd?

After standing in the cold for over an hour, we finally made it to the front of the line. Security let my two friends in and when he got to me, he said the club was over capacity. Since I couldn't get in, my friends weren't going to stay either.

That night turned out to be violent. The next day, we heard from some school friends that a fight broke out in the club shortly after we left. Some guy got put out of the club and shot a gun into the air. What I've learned from this was that we all have a choice and don't have to base our decisions on what others are doing. When I was in college, I wanted to fit in, so I followed along with what others were doing. Now I live doing what I feel is best for me. I allowed myself to say no this isn't for me. Saying no has allowed me to realize it's ok to not follow along with what others are doing and being loyal to yourself is a part of self-love

Part I-

Looking Beyond the Surface

Don't always look on the surface for answers. Some things require a diagnostic. We must dig deeper and search the root of a situation in order to find a solution. When seeds are planted, roots are formed. When roots have been in the ground a long time, the plant becomes deeply rooted and could be entangled with other things. When you search for the root, you will find unresolved issues.

The Test

When things seem to be going against you, remember an airplane takes off against the wind, not with it. The fast air bearing down on a plane generates an upward force on the wings, which helps lift the aircraft. The test is an event or situation that reveals the strength or quality of someone or something by putting them under strain. Just like the airplane, your faith is put to the test by opposing forces. The test can be ongoing and come at constant speed, but as you continue to push forward, it will cause you to grow and elevate to the next level.

I reached a point in my life where I realized I had to stop and take some time to reflect over my life: the mistakes I've made, the misunderstandings I've had, and the hurt that I inflicted on myself. I used those experiences to find my identity and healing. I constantly asked myself, "Who am I? Why so many mistakes? Why did I always take the wrong paths?" For so long, I was in a broken place and didn't know how to work through that. After a lot of soul searching and God seeking, I finally came to a point in my life where I found forgiveness, which led to healing. No matter how many times I questioned myself about my choices, there would never be a suitable answer. What I do know is that it all was working for my good. I realized that the control is not in my hands, but in the hands of the man above and He used those things, the good and the bad. It doesn't always feel that way while going through it, but His promise says otherwise.

A lot of times, we say what we won't do or tolerate, and that is because society has taught us how to live, what to accept, and how life should be. We live under standards but, whose standards? I make sacrifices daily, but I don't always want to. The Bible tells us that God is the rewarder of those who diligently seek Him. I know for a fact that I've allowed others to influence decisions that I've made. I'm thankful that even when I turned to do wrong things, nothing I've done was unseen by God.

I was studying the Book of Ruth, which focuses on the relationship of Ruth and Boaz. I think there are many single women waiting for their Boaz to come sweep her off her feet.

As I studied this book, I asked God to give me fresh insight into His Word and I started to see something entirely different than what I had previously. Ruth's love story is obvious, but I don't think it's the main takeaway. The Book of Ruth was really about Ruth's sacrifice to Naomi, and God's reward to her for it.

In this you will find love, loyalty, and redemption. Ruth and Orpah both married the sons of Ruth and Elimelech. At some point the ladies all lost their spouses and were left alone.

Naomi was too old to have more sons to give Orpah and Ruth possible husbands, and even if she could, the age difference between the women and the young boys would have been an odd sight. They would have been the cougars of the Old Testament. Orpah did the expected things, she kissed her mother in law and set out to return home. Ruth would have returned to her homeland, like Orpah, but she chose to stay with Naomi. Ruth gained a great foundation and learned about God from her mother-in law that she clung to, Naomi.

Therefore, we can assume Ruth's sacrifice to remain with Naomi was out of love, and when we do things out of love, there can be so much more to gain. Had Ruth returned home, like Orpah, would she have found Boaz? Would she have found favor? Would she have walked into her blessing? There is an adage that says, "The bigger the sacrifice, the greater the reward." Ruth gave up an unknown future to provide for and take care of her mother-in-law. Along the way, she found favor with a man and favor with God. When we trust in God's promises, we must block out other people's opinion and thoughts of how life should be lived because it may cause us to lose out on what God has for us. What if Orpah had whispered to Ruth, "Let's get out of here. We can head back home and meet someone great and be remarried"? Or, what if Orpah had told Ruth that she had one ticket in life and that God didn't want her to sacrifice her life and happiness for someone else? What if it was Ruth's desire to be a stay-at-home mom and have a house filled with children? What if Orpah had said something that deterred Ruth from staying with Naomi and Ruth never received what God had in store for her? We've all had those outside inputs from people who advised through their lenses. We managed to know what was best for us.

Understand that other people's opinions about how life should be lived or what standard of living we should seek could cost us our blessing. Be careful of whose advice you take. There may be people telling you that your sacrifices aren't what God wants. Meanwhile, those sacrifices, according to God's promise, are working in your favor. Everyone's life is different, and no one's story will be the same. God isn't the same in our lives. When I share with my friends about situations in my life, I don't always share everything with everyone because I know that everyone isn't on the same level as me and won't be able to receive things the same way I do.

As I ponder over this story of Ruth, I begin to understand more about giving out of a place of love and sacrifice. Ruth loved Naomi, and for the sake of love, went out every day to make sure Naomi was provided for. She never dwelled on what she could have or what she was giving up. She was providing out of love.

I considered Ruth a cheerful giver. I believe that God rewarded her for her sacrifices. None of the ladies in the

Book of Ruth knew what God had in store for them, but the wait is worth it when we trust and wait on God.

I started working when I was fourteen years old. I worked on the weekends with my Aunt Dar cleaning condos in Myrtle Beach. I worked every weekend and if I was out of school on a Friday, I was able to work three days. I was always excited because it was an opportunity to make money. My family didn't have much back then. There were five of us and my working provided more money. I was always a giver, even when I didn't want to be. My family's hardship taught me early on to help when I can, even if there wasn't a lot to give from. There were always sacrifices that I made to help my family, and as I grew older, I felt like I could relate to Ruth. I did what I had to do out of love, even though I didn't know what would come from it; I just did what I needed to do.

By the time I got to high school, things were better. During the summer, I worked two jobs. I was still working with Aunt Dar (she always looked out for me), and my cousin, Sparkle. I started working at a beachwear store at night. We worked all day, 7:30 a.m. to 10 p.m. I still helped out at home, but sometimes, I felt like the more I gave, the more people wanted. I grew bitter because no one gave anything to me, but they wanted every dollar that I had until I was empty again. As an adult, I realized the more money I made, the more problems were going to occur. There were more people in need and more responsibilities came my way.

What if God trusted me with the increase because He wanted to use me? What if God knew He could count on me to take care of those in need? What if God knew I didn't understand what He was doing, but eventually, His plans for my life would be revealed?

There was never a correction to this way of thinking as I grew into adulthood. I grew up still giving from a place of sacrifice. I felt like I was meant to help people, but as a kid I was looking for the reward from it. My parents always told me that I would be rewarded for the things that I did. At some point I stopped believing that because I couldn't see the reward, I came to realize that I was looking for it from the wrong source. As a child, I didn't understand that God was the rewarder of all things. Little did I know, my sacrifices were in His books. Rewards aren't just about money or material things. I received favor and opportunities throughout my life that I could never imagine. Like Ruth there was something greater in store for my sacrifices.

There are two types of pain in the world: pain that hurts you and pain that changes you. I went through a lot of hurt before I reached my change. Years ago, when I told my childhood story, I saw it from a clouded mind. I viewed it through pain. The glass was always empty to me, but really, it was full. It took a renewing of my mind to see it. Regardless of what things looked like I had everything I needed, and God always kept His promise. And even though pain cost me a lot of things, and it took me a longer time than expected to learn from it, things worked out in my favor.

Sometimes, our lessons are tough, but God uses those tough lessons to reveal to us who we really are. I was reminded that when you take on a task or challenges at any capacity you have to be ready to bear the burden that comes along with it. Whatever you say, "Yes" to, just remember you have to be okay with suffering. In the Book of John, Jesus was washing the feet of his disciples, knowing his purpose was about to be fulfilled. He knew the hour was near when things were about to change. The greatest sacrifice ever was about to be fulfilled. Jesus was about to return to the Father. In John 13:7, Jesus said to Peter, "What I'm doing you do not understand now, but you will know after this." From that scripture, I learned that some things must happen a certain way in order for us to reach our destiny and I applied that to my own life journey. Jesus washed the feet of the disciples so that they could be part of Him. He was an example for them. What they have done for others, God will do for them. What God has done for them; they should do for others.

God was teaching me that through what He did for me. Since God will always be my provider, I should help others. In return, what I've done for others, God will do for me. His promises have never failed me. When my parents said that I would be rewarded for all that I do, they were right. I've had doors opened that I didn't deserve to walk through; people gave me chances; people believed in me; they were happy, cheerful, and willing to make sacrifices.

Redefining Love

We love because He first loved us

During one of my sessions, my therapist asked how I defined love. As I sat there with my eye's closed, I couldn't really explain it. I knew love was an intense feeling or a deep affection, but I really didn't have a definition of love. I opened my eyes and gave Dr. Audrey a puzzled look. I didn't know what it meant to me. I hadn't given it much thought. It occurred to me that I didn't have a definition of love because I didn't love me. I never forgave myself for past mistakes. I never fully let go of past pain from old relationships, and I never committed to loving Twanja!

During a spiritual healing session, my instructor asked me to take the four letters of love and share what each letter meant to me.

L stands for Living

O stands for Obedience

V stands for Validation

E stands for Endless

What does that mean? Living a full life, being obedient to God, seeking only God's validation and approval, and receiving an endless amount of forgiveness.

Love is a variety of different feelings, states, and attitudes that range from interpersonal affection to pleasure. Love isn't just a feeling; it is a commitment and a sacrifice. Not everyone will agree with my definition of love because it means something different to everyone, which is fine. I remind myself that God made a promise that He would never leave nor forsake me, and that is His commitment. He sacrificed His son for me—that was His sacrifice. If God made a sacrifice for me, where is my sacrifice to myself?

Hate is the opposite of love. I knew everything that I disliked about myself, but did that mean that I hated myself? I decided to make a list and focus on what I loved about myself. Focusing on the negatives would never change anything. In 2018, there were so many women who reached out to me about how they struggled to make changes with their health, expressing how uncomfortable they felt in their own skin, and wanting change but not knowing how to get there. I understood them because I went through my own depression, where I struggled with the same issues.

For an entire year, I cried getting dressed for work. I changed clothes at least five times every day before I left for work. I would go shopping every week to buy new clothes.

It was a temporary fix, but there was something deeper going on and it was going to take more than new clothes to fix it. I was never comfortable in my own skin. I always wished I could look as cute as the models online while shopping for clothes. One day, I got over what I didn't like and decided to change things. That was when I decided to make changes in my own life. I needed to tackle more than one area. It started with my weight loss journey, which allowed me to see the person I am from within. I began to look at Twanja and realized that I had to love myself no matter what and find value in myself. I went from being unhappy to walking in peace while embarking on a new journey. It was something I had never experienced. If you want to make changes, look directly into your own eyes, dig deeply within yourself, and give yourself all of you. You have to want to become your best and then take steps towards becoming! If God chose you, then you have to choose you too.

Self Love

For so long, I talked about living my best life, but I didn't know how to do that. I was so concerned about helping others live their best lives that I didn't even know what living my best life looked like. For quite some time, I was operating on empty. I always managed to put everyone else first. I came to realize that I couldn't give from a good place if I was empty. That was when I decided to make myself a PRIORITY. I became number one in my life and took care of what I needed. It took some time for me to realize that self-care equals self-love. I don't think I had ever loved, valued, or appreciated myself like I should have. It took a lot of bad experiences and stupidity for me to learn my value and worth. I allowed people to withdraw from me, and there were no deposits made. Along with self-love came boundaries. I finally found the courage to draw a line between myself and anyone who came into my life with the mindset to take up space.

Finally, at the age of thirty-seven, I became free. I am freed from carrying the burdens of others. I finally set limitations on the drama that I allowed to enter my life. I no longer took on other people's problems. I know who I am, and I could no longer burden myself with anything or anyone that could disturb my peace. I have learned to be content with exactly where I am. I no longer live for other people's expectations or standards. I seek God for advice because maybe, just maybe, He is trying to do a new thing through me. No one knows what that looks like, except Him. I no longer sacrifice my peace for others. I have a daily cutoff time, so that I can detox from my day. Once my workday is complete, I don't usually take calls because I need me time. If I'm on the phone while driving on my way home, the conversation ends in the garage. There has to be a cutoff point in order to find balance and live a life of peace. You have to decide what peace looks like for you. Are you able to set boundaries- healthy boundaries that will allow you to give yourself what you need in your season? It could be peace, love, joy, happiness. Whatever that is, only you can control how you get it.

As I learned how to redefine my love, I stumbled across self-love and walked into the direction of living my best life. I had to define what things meant to me in order to discover who I was underneath the surface

Only God Can Validate Me

People often seek validation from others. Social media has taken society's mindset into another realm. People look at "likes" for some type of validation. People crave attention. They wonder if their posts are accepted, worried about putting up something that will make others judge them.

I used to fall into the same trap. I used social media to promote my brand and my business. Before I posted, I would get approvals from my sisters or my coach to make sure that I wasn't saying the wrong things. I was concerned how others would perceive my words. People are so judgmental; it's hard to share anything. Social media has become a place where tearing other people down has become the norm. There is a disregard for other people's feelings. There are no boundaries or respect. You can't be intimate and share your fears or weaknesses because some people will dig into what's left of you and strip you down to nothing. Or the moment you share something that could help someone else people think it is a cry for help.

Instead of focusing on what others thought of me or their reaction to what I did or said, I've learned to focus more on what God is doing through me and what he wants to do in my life. Sometimes, my comments and realizations may not be towards anyone; the battle can be within my own two ears. I can become my own downfall and critic. I've concluded that only God can validate me. He knows my heart and my intentions. I can't change how people treat me or act towards me. I can only control my reactions and the way I treat others. I had to learn this, and it took some time for me to truly understand it. I have to be careful how I treat others because the seeds that I plant, the words that I speak, and the actions that I take will create a harvest. Whatever comes back to me, I better be sure I can live with it..

Endless

Have you ever been in a relationship with someone who grew tired of your habits or ways and ended the relationship? Have you ever thought about whether or not God gets tired of you? Would He say I'm done with you? What if God says, "No more; you don't listen," then tells you everything that you've done wrong? Have you ever feared that God would leave you like the last person did? I think everyone has had a moment in life where they wonder if God still loves them the same way or may have questioned his love. I've asked so many times, "God, why are you still good to me when I don't deserve it?" Life can take us to some low points, and we may measure the love of others and compare it to God's. I know that God loves me enough to provide me with more than enough chances. He gives us unlimited chances.

A few years ago, I went on a spiritual retreat called Healing the Heart. This weekend getaway was the beginning of God gutting out my inner core. I was broken and badly in need of healing. I arrived knowing that I was meeting God at the shack. I knew that if I could just get there, He would show up. A month before I went on the retreat, I felt healed from the pain I endured from a recent breakup. I told myself that I was in a good place and didn't need to go. I was starting to feel a temporary false sense of peace. I was starting to believe that I was OK, but I knew what would take place once I got there. I arrived with expectancy. I was determined to receive God's peace and it was waiting for me to show up and accept it.

Let me take a minute to describe God's peace. It was everything the Book of Psalms described in chapter twenty-three. God was my shepherd and he knew exactly what I needed. The place He brought me was enormous with green pastures. God led me to a place that brought rest to my soul, and He led me beside still water God allowed me to be still as He restored my strength and soul at the retreat. I'm not saying I was totally healed, but in that place, I was in God's presence and I sensed His peace. This was the beginning of a pivotal moment in my life. There was a time to openly share, a time to be still, and a time to hear from God.

After all the stops, turns, and getting off track, I finally felt like I was headed towards healing. There was pain, but did you know purpose is to be birthed out of pain? While pain is never comfortable, it is even more difficult to bear when it comes unexpectedly because we are unprepared.

If no one around you has been through what you've gone through, no one can offer comfort in your affliction. You might feel unsure about whether the intensity of the hurt is a common thing. You might wonder what you should do in response to it. Often, I've felt alone while going through my struggles. I've felt like my life was jacked up when I was open and transparent, but everyone else kept their pain a secret. Just so you know that you don't have to isolate yourself while going through your challenges. Everyone faces struggles; some are just more transparent and open about them. None of us can go through life pain-free. We all go through setbacks, go through difficult times, and even cry— sometimes cry a lot. No matter what you are facing, know that we are not supposed to do life alone. It is encouraging to know that you are walking with someone.

Self-Love

Have you ever looked in the mirror and told yourself: I love you or I love who you are? I haven't. When I started taking care of myself mentally and physically, I started to enjoy spending time with myself. I stopped searching for external things that only create an illusion of fulfilling my emptiness.

Finding Love Within
(Am I Good Enough?)

Self-love is something I knew nothing about. I've learned that self-love goes hand and hand with healing. Instead of finding the things I didn't love about me, I wanted to discover the things that were unique about me. I needed to know the things that set me apart, the things that defined me, the things that made me who I am. If I focused on the things I didn't love about myself or the hurt and pain I suffered, I would have continued to walk around broken. There is no healing in misery and there is no healing when you can't let go of your past.

During the first half of my life, I held onto the pain of everything that bothered me about myself. I had to get beyond that. I had to escape the criticism that would appear suddenly in my head. I found the answer in the Serenity Prayer:

"O God, give us the serenity to accept what cannot be changed, the courage to change what can be changed, and the wisdom to know the difference." –Reinhold Niebuhr

I've struggled with identity issues. Growing up, I

didn't fit in with the in-crowd. I struggled with my weight all my life and I had low self-esteem. I've always had people in my life who called themselves my "friends," but talked badly about me. I guess that wasn't really friendship. Whenever I liked someone, they always chose someone else over me. That didn't help with my self-esteem. I wondered why I wasn't good enough. I never went on a date when I was in high school. I always saw people in relationships and waited for my guy to show up. He never did. It was tough for me because I had no one to confide in or express what I was feeling. I felt different, like an outcast. I would watch my sister get all dolled up and pretty with her makeup. She had guys who liked her, but I was always picked over. I felt like a misfit, and the hurtful part was the paranoia of thinking that every time I walked into a room, people were going to talk about me. It was all in my head.

Once I did start dating, I still wasn't good enough. I was in dead-end relationships and allowed the other person to cheat on me. Once, I dated this guy named Seth. In the beginning, he would go missing. I wouldn't hear from him for days. Come to find out, he had met me and another girl around the same time, and he was going back and forth between the both of us. Three months in, she ended up pregnant. He left me to do the right thing for his child. Eventually, he left her because it didn't work, and he ran back to me. I took him back, but he was filled with drama. He was a player and there were more women throughout our entire relationship.

We went back and forth for years until I eventually had enough of him. He told me the very thing I had been feeling inside for so many years—that I wasn't good enough. He said I was never anything to him and the moment he figured it out, he didn't want anything to do with me. I knew it wasn't the truth, but his words broke my spirit down. I had felt that way for so long about myself. Something about hearing those words out loud shattered my spirit, and no matter how many friends told me that he wasn't good enough for me, the idea that I wasn't good enough echoed in my head. It wasn't the first time someone had said it. Once, I was friends with another guy and his family was a little uppity. We were on the phone one day and I heard his mom in the background, talking negatively about me. I hadn't even met her, but she was saying I wasn't good enough for her son.

I could go on and on with my pity party, but the truth is, I was more than enough. Those people just weren't supposed to be in my life.

I realized I was never taught how to love myself. All I saw was my flaws and how I didn't fit in. No one ever told me I didn't have to fit in. I didn't understand what was meant by beauty only being skin deep. I never realized that I needed to love who I am the way that God created me. My spirit and soul were more important than my flesh. I just wished that someone had taught me how to value myself at that time. I wish someone had taught me that flaws are minor, and we all have them. I wish I would have opened up and talked to someone about my feelings.

No one is perfect, but no matter what I do, how I look, what I am, God loves me. It took me a while to realize that I am a beauty queen and deserve nothing but the best. I am smart; I am intelligent; I am lovable; I am God's creation and everything he created was good. That is what I want you to know about yourself. You are worth it; you are beautiful; and you don't need anyone to validate that. The right person will see you at the right time and that person will see your heart and not just your surface.

Sometimes, it might seem like our world is crumbling. God's Word says, "Weeping may endure for a night, but joy comes in the morning." God won't allow us to stay in our situation. Life can be full of painful situations, but the eyes of faith will see outside the boundaries of these situations to the bigger picture beyond.

Throughout the course of my life, there were times when I would shy away from the thought of being used by God. I wanted to learn more about the Word, but I didn't quite understand God's love for me. I went back and forth in my relationship with God, like a ping pong ball, and I never fully committed. Whenever I drew closer to God and started to build a relationship with Him, I was always sidetracked with distractions. I magnified my relationships with people and focused less on building a relationship with God. I allowed people to become more important to me. I valued their opinions and thoughts, but not what God said about me. I was looking for something I never had but looking at the wrong source to receive it. I dedicated too much time pleasing people and being a part of something that could never fill me up. In my mind, I knew God, but my flesh was on the hunt of its own. I focused on building a career, getting a title, making money, and not to mention, dead-end relationships. I wanted something I never had. I wanted someone to validate who I was, to make me feel like I was worth valuing. I was living reckless for people, when all along God's love was reckless for me.

I placed myself in relationships that deteriorated my self-esteem. These relationships taught me some tough lessons. They allowed me to get to the root of underlying issues. My relationship with Alex is a perfect example of this. In the beginning, Alex was "the one." He was the first guy I was in a relationship with, but I was more committed to the relationship than he was. I worked so hard to make the relationship succeed, it sucked the life out of me. I so desperately wanted to have someone in my life that I just accepted what came along with it. Like many women, I thought if I did more and more for my man, he would someday see that I was good enough, desirable, and just maybe, he would want to reciprocate by treating me better. That never happened for me, and it likely doesn't work for anyone. No matter how much I prayed, he never changed, and neither did I. He was still an alcoholic, still on and off jobs, and was still running around with different women. How could I expect anyone to see my worth or the value of me when I didn't even see it?

I found myself trying to help someone who didn't want to help himself. Alex didn't know how to love himself and didn't know how to love me. People say they know what love is, but when we break it all down, do we really? People overlook and tolerate a lot of things that they shouldn't do out of love.

Finally, I reached a point where I didn't want to be in that situation with Alex anymore and it was time to part ways. I prayed that God would bring separation between us. It didn't end pretty. His words were hurtful, but I think those painful words opened my eyes and kept me from going back.

We had broken up before and it was never really over, but that time, I felt closure. I knew I would never look back. I finally knew that it would only get better when I realized that I no longer needed to allow people in my life who didn't have good intentions for me. I understood that there are people and things in life that aren't meant to stay. Sometimes, change may not be what we want now, but exactly what we need.

I knew I needed to change my life as badly as I needed to breathe each day to stay alive, but I didn't know how relationships could become addictive. There is a compelling need to connect with and remain connected with a person. We run to them again and again, looking to be accepted or to fill an empty void. Emotional addictions are no different than breaking a habit of overindulging or overeating. An emotional attachment requires great willpower to leave. Fortunately, my experience forged me into a strong woman. That relationship was overdue for an ending. Alex's last words to me—that I was never good enough for him—were exactly what I needed to hear. I suffered a lot of pain and guilt, but I was able to get through those bad times. I cried many days and nights because I was so disappointed in myself. I wish I could say after this that I forgave myself, but unfortunately, I moved on without healing properly. I ended up creating more damage to myself as the years progressed. I never addressed the issue. I allowed myself to suppress the pain, so that I could move on. For years, I learned to function with pain that I had allowed to become dormant and eventually, it resurfaced.

There are two types of pain in the world: pain that hurts and pain that changes us. In my situation, I endured both types of pain. I learned, I grew, and I moved on. It wasn't easy and I was stuck, but I wanted better for myself and I deserved better. The type of pain that I experienced made me change my outlook on life, people, and myself.

I struggled to share my story because I didn't want people to know the areas I struggled with. I couldn't look myself in the mirror, knowing that I failed. I worked diligently building my career and chasing my dreams. I have several degrees, but I failed when it came to love. I felt embarrassed by the relationships that I allowed myself to be in for many years. I felt down because I had wasted so many years that I couldn't get back and most of my friends were already married. I used to replay in my head how foolish I was for allowing the words of my ex to affect me the way that they did. I knew what he said wasn't true, but I couldn't move past it.

Eventually, I came to terms with the fact that the very experiences that had caused me to hurt allowed me to grow. I didn't want to share my flaws with anyone because I was so concerned about what people would say or how they would perceive me. I had to realize that the very thing that I had experienced and learned from could help someone else find freedom and forgiveness. I had to let go of the things that were behind me and set myself free. Now, I remind myself every day that I am a prize, and I will not let people put me in a place that I don't want to be in. I needed to see myself as a diamond, even if I was rough around the edges.

Throughout all of this, I've learned that change was vital for me to become the person that I saw myself. Change takes place when pressure is applied. You don't have to beat yourself up when things aren't going the way you feel it should. I even learned not to rush anything because things happen at an appointed time. It takes strength and courage to admit the truth and admitting my truth has allowed me to heal.

Handling the Truth

When we learn to be open, the truth follows. The truth always reveals itself in time. I thought that most people lived in a perfect bubble because that is what people wanted me to see. I had to learn that I don't know what page of life people are on, but my own experience taught me differently. I was the person who was dying inside. I was in pain with unanswered questions, crying out to God, asking Him if I had to drink from this cup.

There were times when I thought I was alone in my battles; I was not. I realize now that there are many others hurting just like I was internally. I felt alone. Some people want others to see their "After," but don't realize that the power is in the "Before." The truth isn't polite, popular, or pretty. We must own our truth and accept it for what it is, so that we can move on. We can try to cover things up and hide our scars because we don't like who we are. Everyone has something they struggle with, stuff they aren't proud of, but so what. It makes us who we are. This book is about me owning my truth and setting myself free in hopes of being a reflection for someone else.

As I process my experiences, I become self-aware. Self-awareness is significant because when we have a better understanding of ourselves, we can experience ourselves as unique and separate individuals. I became empowered to make required changes and to build on my areas of strength as well as identify areas where I need to make additional improvements. I learned how to confront the demon that was in my blind spot—my lack of understanding and impartiality.

When I graduated from college back in 2003, I was a Unit Manager at the Waffle House. At age twenty-three, I was managing a staff between twenty and thirty employees. It was a tough job. I had people from all walks of life. I remember there was one part-time employee named Susan. She had another full-time job in Human Resources for a plant in Charlotte, NC. Susan needed the extra money to help one of her kids who was going through a tough time. During the holidays back then, it was very busy. Waffle House was the only restaurant open on Christmas Day in our area. The lines were very long. The wait would be more than an hour, but the tables turned over quickly.

In the middle of the rush, Susan came to me, panicking that she couldn't do it. Her anxiety was up high, and she was about to shut down. She, like many of us, let what was going on around her carry more weight than it should. My advice to her was to focus on what was in front of her and pretend that nothing else mattered. I told her to keep her eyes on what was ahead and let nothing else distract her. It doesn't sound easy to do, but it becomes easier with practice. Sometimes, we have to focus on the task and not let stress take over. In life, we must acknowledge circumstances when they arise, but we can't lose sight of everything else we have going on because something happens.

Sarah Jakes Roberts once said, "Your life will go in the direction you are looking." So, keep your eyes on the road. Your attention will affect your driving direction. Whatever you give your attention to is what you will unconsciously gravitate towards. If your attention is going to the right, your body is going to the right. Ms. Roberts said that "if you ever want to know which way you are looking, monitor what you are saying. Your mouth is telling you what your heart is seeing." The things that we talk about and rage about are stopping us from being who we were created to be.

When the Truth Shows Up—Searching Deep Within

You have everything you need to live a life of true fulfillment. Everything you need for your destiny is within reach. I believe that people are assigned to our journey, and God will give me eyes to recognize opportunities, people, and resources that he has placed in my life to further His plan for me.

The phrase "allowing your truth to show up" refers to being honest with yourself and facing those past hurts. You have to face the things that keep you in a place of fear and hold you back from living your dreams. Living your dream requires you to fight for an opportunity rather than allowing your past struggles to stop you from being the person you want to be. It won't always be easy, but it gets better with time. A little progress each day can turn into big results – if you don't give up. Sometimes, we focus more on the end results and think it is too far fetched when we should enjoy the process. No matter how many times I've made mistakes, nothing could keep me from being the person I'm called to be, which brings joy to me. It's so easy to find fault in ourselves and to blame ourselves for things we can't erase. I used to think that because of my wrongdoings or mistakes, that I could never become great and that I would be stuck, but that isn't what God does. He sees beyond our past, pains, and struggles, and allows us to see what He created in us. He still uses us despite our history. God doesn't see history. He sees me and it's time that I see myself as well.

When I reflect on my weight, I wondered why my parents allowed me to become overweight. I wondered why they never disciplined my eating habits. Why didn't they stop me from unhealthy choices? Why didn't they teach me more about what being overweight would do to me mentally? I don't blame them because at some point, I made my own choices. I didn't understand the concept of being healthy and making better choices. Eventually, I figured it out, but it cost me a lot. I never went on dates, my self-esteem was very low, and I never saw passed my weight. I also struggled with the fear of rejection, unworthiness, humiliation, overindulgence, depression, and low self-esteem.

Life comes with challenges that may knock us down, but we all need to see how other people managed to live their dreams, despite the giants that stood in their paths. There are many ways to success, and we must keep in mind that there isn't a right or wrong path. You can do all things, if you believe in yourself and allow yourself to be open for guidance. You can choose to change anytime you want; the choice is yours.

Often, we look for happiness in things or in other people. I most certainly have. The truth is that happiness is something I have to create internally. It comes from making wise choices, including to be happy. You can choose to be happy even when things are not going the way you expect it to. It took years of failing to understand that I control my own happiness. I had to learn that concept the hard way. Pain and heartbreak forced me to pay more attention to myself. I had to spend a great amount of time processing my life, my mistakes, thinking about what's next in my life, and really asking God why things happened as they did. Lord, why did this happen or that happen? Did I learn what was needed from it? I was taught that when you know the reasons behind things, comprehension is clearer.

I used to overlook things in my relationships. Now, I realize that if I had just listened, I would have learned everything I needed to know was within me. The Latin word, introspicere, means "to look inside. Introspection is when we examine how what we do, say, think, and feel affect our lives and the lives of others. How often do you self-reflect and search deep within to discover the person that you are? I found there isn't anything wrong with thinking about myself more and calculating my own interest; it's more like searching inside in order to understand myself. When I chose to become self-observing, I spent a considerable amount of time examining my own thoughts and feelings. I had to specifically contemplate myself. I've been told that I think too much or over analyze everything. I found this to be one of my greatest strengths. My life has been a constant reflection of me trying to find my inner beauty.

The very first book that I wrote was called Led by the Word. It allowed me to share testimonies about my life struggles. The older I get, the more I've grown into understanding things differently. The glass could be half empty or half full; however, you decide to look at it as your own choice. I was trapped in bad thoughts for years that I allowed to replay over and over again. I finally realized there is no good in holding onto negative thoughts. No good comes from constantly thinking about the past. In order to move forward, I had to change the sound. I once heard someone say, that there is a sound that precedes the movement of God. In order for something positive to come out of a bad memory, thought, or experience, we have to view how we are perceiving it. Anything could change if you switch up the beat. I like to think of this new beginning in my life as healing from my past darkness. I grew up thinking about the struggle and how we didn't have much, but I was rich in other things. I could only be rich if I saw myself beyond my struggle. I may not have what I want now, but nothing is stopping me from getting it. I have everything I need to manifest the things I desire.

My family taught me about survival and how to make it through hard times. My parents showed us how to make a little stretch into enough. My aunts took me to church, so that I would learn about God and that allowed the Word to root inside me. I grew up in a community where everyone knew each other, and the people were always giving. I believe that is part of the reason why I'm a giver. It was instilled in me since my youth. My grandmother taught me how to pray. She told me that the Lord was my shepherd and I shall not want. She was right. He has been a light whenever I faced dark times. During the down periods in my life, growth was able to take place because of those early lessons. That is where the work is. Anyone can have faith or be positive when life is going their way. The real challenge of growing mentally, emotionally, and spiritually comes when you get knocked down. Adversity introduces us to ourselves. How you handle adversity is where growth takes place.

Principles to Live By

There are great timeless principles out there that have changed the lives of many people. Usually, a timeless principle is something that someone discovers in their own life and realizes it can be true for others

Obedience and Understanding

Obedience, in human behavior, is the ability to carry out commands. Obedience to God is very significant in our walk with Christ. Not one person in this lifetime will ever become sufficiently sanctified to the point where they are always obeying the law, but we can honor and maintain obedience to God by pondering, or meditating on, the words of Jesus and trying to obey. In the book of John 14:23 Jesus spoke to the people and said anyone who loves me will obey my teaching. My father will love them, and we will come to them and make our home with them

When we are being obedient to God, we are doing just that: knowing Him, loving Him, and having a personal, intimate relationship with Him to fully understand and obey what He is asking of us. Obedience is letting God set the direction, even if He doesn't give the details. We have to understand that He knows what's best for us.

God promised that when we walk in obedience with His commanding, we will live, prosper, and prolong our days in the land that we possess.

It's difficult to obey something we don't understand or better yet, to obey a commandment when we don't understand the reasons it was given. Sometimes, we have to realize that God will take us through things even when we have no idea what He is doing in our lives. We can't see what God sees or know what He is doing. All we can do is put our trust in Him because there is a greater purpose that is unforeseen. In the end, it helps to mold us into the person He wants us to be and it allows us to see who God really is. It builds character and faith.

A few years ago, I worked in retail management. I was exhausted with my position, so I kept praying to God, telling Him that I wanted to leave. At the time, I was also in school and I had bills to pay, so the fear of losing what I had kept me in my position. Fear of the unknown will keep a person tied to a place or in a season. God was telling me to trust in Him and step out on faith, but I was making good money, had no children, and I worried about leaving when I didn't have another job secured. One day, I finally asked myself why I worked. Was I working to build a better life for myself? Was it for financial stability? Was it to afford the things that I didn't have? Or, was it to help my family out because they depended on me? Either way, I wasn't happy.

The more I contemplated stepping out in faith, the more I thought about how much I needed my job. I stayed because of the money and because of fear. During that time, I was willing to sacrifice my happiness for security.

Then, out of nowhere, financial hardship hit. My salary plummeted. I was very frustrated and emotionally disturbed. My parents helped me out a lot and that bothered me, but eventually, I realized that I was blessed that they were able to sow into my season. This was a blessing not a handout. I felt like not stepping out on faith portrayed insubordination and fear. I feared failure and that caused me not to trust God.

My life began to feel like a whirlwind, like things were spinning out of control. My health was beginning to suffer due to the way I was living. I had allowed stress to take over. I had no choice but to leave my job. So much had happened to me so suddenly. I had an ulcer, a bulging disc in my lower back, and a torn meniscus.

It wasn't until after my surgery that I did what I felt led to do—be obedient to the Spirit. I walked away in faith, and I knew in my heart that I had made the right choice. In spite of what I had to go through to walk away, I realized that in order for something to begin, something had to end. Change is difficult, but it is necessary. Once I made moves, I became more confident in my decision and began to feel a sense of peace come over me.

A very good friend once told me that life is all about taking chances, so I set out to discover something new about myself. I was looking for my purpose and was determined to seek God's plan for my life. If everything had been wrong, it had to go right. I now realize that my season was changing, but I wasn't. Don't walk into fall dressed like summer. You have to be able to recognize the shift and change with your season.

No matter how hard you try, you can't predict what

will happen. After leaving my job and recovering from the surgery, I needed time to rest and heal. I knew it was time to gain order and become more purpose-driven, but mainly, hit the reset button. I knew I wanted to grow closer, so I began going to Wednesday Bible Study and regular service. I committed my heart and mind. I made up my mind that I would do whatever it took. I wanted to learn more about God's love for me.

It was time that I figured out who I was. It's like learning your family history. I asked questions and I learned the greatest stories. My first question was: Who am I? I'm not talking about my name or my parents; it goes a little deeper. In everything that we do, there is a vision, right? If I was going to open a business, there would be a plan for that business. There would be purpose, and it would meet a demand and a need for someone or something. So, what about my life? What is the purpose of me being here? What do I have that would benefit others? How can I bring change? All these questions have an answer. God must have thought about His vision and plan before I came to the earth. All I must do is figure it all out. Where does He want me to go?

I wanted to hear from God, but most importantly, I wanted to know my purpose. What did I have to contribute to others? How could I become an answer to someone's problem? I wanted to become a window, so that God would pour out His blessing through me. Instead of focusing on why God wanted to use me, I asked myself why not me? I no longer wanted to be stuck believing I wasn't good enough because I am more than enough, and I wanted to make myself available for God to use me to do His will. I began to pray and seek God. I began to pray for wisdom and direction. Something was moving inside of me, something was changing in my thought process, and I started to feel divergent. I knew deep down that I would do whatever it took to do God's will. I still have my flaws, but that doesn't change the way God feels about me. Nothing I could do would change the way God sees me. He just had to get me to see myself the way that He does. I'm not picture perfect, but I was made complete. "And in Christ you have been brought to fullness. He is the head over every power and authority" (Colossians 2:10). The width of God's love extends across the entire world and includes all people, everyone He has created.

If God loves you, why does it matter what anybody else thinks? Because God loves you, there's no need to prove your self-worth. John 3:16 says, God loves the whole world. We don't need props anymore to make us feel good about ourselves. We don't have to wear certain kinds of clothes to make us feel like we're okay or drive a certain kind of car to prop up our faltering egos. We don't need status symbols anymore. And we don't have to live our lives the way others feel we should. God sees beyond the mascara. He wipes off the MAC makeup. He knows the reason why we make those mistakes. He understands us when we say that we are sorry for our wrongdoing. He knows our struggles and where we are in life. When people are trying to tear you down, allow the love of God to build you back up.

As I continued to grow, I believed that my life would come together as long as I continued to seek God, remain positive when things didn't make any sense, and trust Him when He said that He would never leave nor forsake me.

I felt like I was beginning to connect with God. Things were becoming clearer, and I was finally on the path to understanding His love for me. All of the doubt was beginning to dissipate.

I started listening while God spoke to me. I had to keep a pen and paper handy. God showed me visions through dreams, and I would write them down. I carried around my notepad and pen just in case God shared anything pertaining to making my life become better. I took notes so I could study what I believed He was saying. I asked myself, "How could I carry out a task, an assignment, His word? I thought I needed to be special. There needed to be something special about me—what was it, though? In my mind, I had all the answers: I knew God loved me; I knew He used people. He'd use them even if they had issues, at least He did in the Bible, but where did Twanja fit in with all of that?

When I began to hear God, I was still building an intimate relationship with Him. As I grew more and more in Christ, I became deeply amazed. I'm not saying it wasn't hard to do things God's way, and in the beginning, I found it hard to fully trust something I didn't understand. It's easy to say, "God, I trust you…" until situations arise, and you really have to trust Him. I had to learn that it's all about growth and moving on another level. Often, things won't register for us because we were taught to live our lives a certain way. We try to understand everything that we do. It is written that we are to "trust in the LORD with all your heart and lean not on your own understanding" (Proverbs 3:5).

He gave us reasons why we should believe in Him, and He even gave us examples. I've learned that no matter how hard things get, I should focus on God. It takes patience and endurance to get to that point. In Hebrews 5:8, it says that Jesus learned obedience through the things He suffered.

When I broke up with my ex-boyfriend, I felt so much pain spreading across my chest. It was excruciating. This pain was unlike a burn or a cut, where there's a physical scar to see the source of my discomfort. This pain was inside of me. It was the pain that comes when we lose someone we love. It was the kind of pain that makes it hard to get out of bed and face the day. I wanted to just lay there and cry. It was the pain of detachment, when someone tied to you is ripped away. There were so many emotions attached to that pain: hurt, fear, guilt, and embarrassment.

Whenever I deal with a heartbreaking pain, I envision the love of God and pretend that I am curled up in His arms. I wanted to feel God's protection. I wanted to let go of my feelings, let my guard down, and confront my pain.

I needed to allow myself to know it would be ok again someday. I would cry out to God, knowing I would be safe in His arms. I poured out every ounce of my emotions because I knew He would hear me. My relationship with God is still developing. Through my growth with God, I've become more reliant on Him and less on myself.

I've learned to focus only on the things that I could control. It was not benefiting me, wanting others to treat me the way I treated them. It became taxing to my health, wanting people to do better or become more. I had to really think about living my life for me and just become an example that maybe others would want to follow. That is the only change I could provide.

Even Abraham Made Sacrifices

When I hear the word "sacrifice," I immediately wonder, "What am I giving up?" What am I willing to pay a price for? People willingly make sacrifices for the things that are important to them.

In Genesis, God puts Abraham through a test. He challenges Abraham to sacrifice his son, Isaac, for the Lord, and Abraham almost does it! Luckily for Isaac, God tells Abraham not to go through with it at the last minute (NIV, Gen. 2-9). Can you imagine what Abraham was feeling? He was willing to sacrifice his own precious son to be obedient to the word of God. It's clear that putting God first and doing His will was important to Abraham. What a test! We never know what God may ask us to let go of. When I think of that sacrifice, I think of Abraham's faith, obedience, and commitment to God. I can't begin to fathom what was running through Isaac's mind.

For most of my life, I've faced challenges that have helped me to develop into the person that I am today. I hope you can see that from all of the stories that I've shared with you. There will be trials and tribulations that we will face on our journey. It wasn't easy for me, but the more confident I became in understanding life, the easier things became. I realized that my faith on one level had to be different on the next. I had to remember how God brought me through the last situation when I didn't know how He would do it. I reaffirmed for myself that if He did it before, He would do it again. There were times when I had to meditate on His words, literally murmuring His Word, and regurgitated to myself that everything was in His control.

Everyone faces trials; no one is exempt from problems. Money can resolve issues, but it can also attach burdens to it. We all have problems that we deal with on a day-to-day basis. When I think of Michael Jackson's song, "You Are Not Alone," I realize that I am not alone in my walk. I am not alone in my struggles, and I am not alone on this journey called life. Everything I need was planted for me to find as I continue to press forward.

While recovering from a back injury, stomach surgery, knee surgery, and an ulcer, I hit some ups and down periods. I know how it feels when life is up and I have everything I need, but I also know how it feels when things are down. It's scary and stressful and hard, but I still had everything I needed.

When I was taking time for my right knee to recover from surgery, my left knee began to cause me pain. Taking the year off was the best decision I could have ever made. I had downtime to restore the strength in my body from all the pain, but I could also focus on where my life was heading. The downside was not having enough income. Those hard times of not being able to make ends meet and barely getting by was an indication that I wanted more for my life.

 This was a time when I drew closer and closer to God, still not understanding, but seeking after His promise.

I knew that I had to want change in order for change to occur. Those tough moments that break you down are the moments when we decide our direction. I always knew that I wanted to be Oprah's successor. I don't want to be Ms. Oprah Winfrey; Twanja Windley is who I am. I just wanted to be a blessing to others. I wanted to be able to bring joy to people's lives. I was at my lowest and I couldn't stop thinking about helping others become better. I knew my community needed me. I looked at my struggles: government assistance, sleeping in the dark for a week because my lights were turned off, or not having groceries and I was determined I would have a better future. Just from hearing stories of others, I knew that they pushed through their hardship, so I had to keep pushing. I began to adapt an abundant mindset: I am rich; I will always have more than enough. This isn't the end of my life and things will get better. My pastor shared with us that pain is never without purpose. Our pain would move us in the direction of our dreams. I just had to remember that my seasons weren't my life because seasons change. I had to believe that I wouldn't be in that place for long.

And may you have the power to understand, as all God's people should, how wide, how long, how high, and how deep his love is. May you experience the love of Christ, though it is too great to understand fully. Then you will be made complete with all the fullness of life and power that comes from God. (Ephesians 3:18-19)

God was teaching me some things, but at the same time, I had to be tested to see if I was ready. Things started to get a little more intense. It felt like the heat was turned up and so had my faith. I would cry out to God for comfort and He would give me understanding as I continued to seek Him. He assured me that He was there with a sense of peace; and I knew I wasn't alone. I was nervous, but brave.

I could not take my eyes off God. I also needed to keep my head clear, so I could finish up my degree. I realized I had to stand up to my problems, so I could come out of my situation. This was my opportunity to build success, and in my mind, I could never give up.

Change can be one of the biggest challenges in life. It is easy to become complacent but challenging to embrace new beginnings. Change can be hard to accept because it disrupts your comfort zone and the norm. I wanted change, but I wanted to change and still be comfortable. Change found me when I decided that I wanted something different. I changed my life by changing my mindset. I could have focused on everything that went wrong, but instead; I chose to focus on what was next. I can't go back and change what happened, and a pity party wouldn't help me. Sometimes, things may look dysfunctional, out of order, and you can't see your way, but God never goes back on His promises. You may not be able to see where you are going, but your steps are ordered. I knew I didn't want to quit school, but I also realized that some huge sacrifices were required. I had to decide to drop out of school or keep pressing. I was preparing for something greater, and at that time, I was six months away from graduating. I wasn't sure what I was supposed to do. It was overwhelming. I moved back home with my parents. On the days I had to go to school, I would drive two hours to my sister's house and drive an hour and a half to go to school or work. I was taking night classes. There were times when I would get a room at a hotel or stay with one of my best friends, who always opened his home and welcomed me in. I didn't earn much money working part-time and most of it was used in gas to commute back and forth.

One day, I didn't have anything to eat. It took everything I had to fill up on gas. I was too ashamed to ask my friends. I felt as if I failed, and I didn't want to hear that I had made a mistake. After class one night, I remembered that I had ten dollars on my EBT. All I could do was cry. It felt as if I was on an emotional roller coaster. I had become financially unstable in less than a year. I had no idea where I was going or what was next. I went to BI-LO and got a bottle of water, a sandwich, and a can of Pringles. I saved half the sandwich for the next day. I rode around with my clothes in my car. I felt lost but determined. I thanked God for strengthening me during those shameful moments. You will never know what you can do unless you try. It all comes down to what you are willing to sacrifice.

As I pondered over my situation, I began to understand how people who lost their homes and had to live in their cars felt. I rode around, knowing that my car was all I had. Although I didn't have to sleep in my car, I felt empty inside, lost and alone. I was an adult and I should be providing for myself. I thought I was hopeless. All of my friends were making money and pressing forward in their careers. I almost questioned my decision to step out on faith and keep going. There were many thoughts that crossed my mind. I never stopped to realize that I was a work in progress. I still wonder about the choices I made and why, but when I reflect on yesterday, I tell myself that when you make choices you have to ride it all the way out so that you are able to see what you gain from it. When I think about it, I had to know how other people felt. I had to put my feet in their shoes and walk their journey to understand where I was going. I've been asking to become a giver, but I needed to see firsthand what that need felt like and why I needed to help. I needed to be able to empathize with what others go through. My strongest take away from this is nothing can stop what is in the plans for you.

 Sometimes you have to let your circumstances know that what things appear to look like isn't always reality. I can only manage what I have and whatever I don't have, I will trust in God to handle it. I can do what I can with the things in my control, whatever is out of my control, I will trust in God to handle it. He would never ask me to do something outside of my ability. I lost a lot throughout this time: my job and my apartment. It was chaotic, but I kept on going, knowing that God would provide just like He said He would. After all of the things I had to endure, God blessed me with over $30,000 unexpectedly. I had more than enough money to get my life back on track; I found another place to stay; and paid the rent out for six months while I completed school. I slipped and fell going into a building. There wasn't a wet sign up, but luckily, there were witnesses and a camera. What I've endured through my journey was indescribable. I went from not having any money to having more than enough money.

Have you ever just given something your all and watched things fall right before your eyes? You couldn't understand why it wasn't working out no matter how much effort you used

I struggled getting my master's degree. There were so many reasons why I should have quit, but there was one reason why I kept going. God was bigger than any mountain that stood in my way. I knew that if I could see beyond my current situation and keep my eyes on the finish line, in spite of what was in front of me, I would obtain my goals.

Become the Change

When I think of the phrase "become the change," I think it means to begin to be different. You should set yourself apart and become what you want to see. As I started thinking about how to change my outlook on life, I had to ask myself what my goals were. What goals should I set? Who was I representing and fighting for? What would such change look like through my eyes? Through much reflection, I realized that who I am is not about what I see, but rather, how I perceive myself. My life is a reflection of my thinking and it cannot be changed until I change my thoughts.

I worked countless hours for about seven years in the automotive industry, chasing what I thought was success. I was living a miserable life. I gave my all into my work, hoping to climb the ladder. I took every negative thing that came along with it: being overlooked for positions that I was qualified for; being told I could never get a certain position because I was a woman; being told I could never become a manager because I was a black woman. I was knocked down so many times, so I fought harder to prove myself, and for what? So that every woman of color would be able to have a voice, an opportunity, and to see that they can become whatever their hearts desired. We deserved to have the same opportunity and rights as everyone else. I fought so hard to be heard and I won't allow anyone else to write or tell my story. No one should dictate the trajectory of our lives.

There was a time when I was fired from my job, and my former employer tried to devalue my work performance. I had been in the same career field for quite some time, so I understood my job. I'm a workaholic and I love to learn new things. Knowledge is something no one can take from me. I aimed to be my absolute best. I put my all into my work because I wanted my work to stand out. People look up to me and it is hard for me to let them down. So many people believe in me and root for me to do good. I don't take anything I do for granted because I'm honored that I get the opportunity to do it.

I was unfairly treated and dismissed, and the sorriest excuse provided was that my work wasn't good enough. I've never heard anything like that in all of my years. I started working when I was fourteen years old. I had some of the best managers who taught me about business. I was always sought after and increased my pay by ten thousand dollars each year. I put seven years into that field, but as I was picking up the pieces, it made me think about my life. I feel in some cases, women don't get the respect, the attention, the adequate pay, or the equal rights that we deserve. We can't get the same jobs and still have to fight for opportunities.

Over the years, I've seen it happen to many people. Being fired from your job is never an easy thing to face, especially after sacrificing everything and giving your all. I walked away with my head held high because I was tired of proving myself or my worth to others. I was calm and disappointed. I was confused and happy. For a second, I had a Waiting to Exhale moment. Seven whole years, I sacrificed, and you can fire me at the drop of a dime. I packed up my things and walked out. I should have left that field a long time ago. My emotions were all over the place, and I was disappointed by all of the underhanded stuff that took place. I had to constantly remind myself that God said vengeance is His (Romans 12:19). Relief set in because I had been freed. That job was a place that I had served that didn't appreciate what I brought to the table. Even though I had been forced out, I was finally staring change in the face. It was a change that I was afraid to make on my own. It felt like the universe had pushed me out of my comfort zone, so that I could push into my purpose. I wasn't walking away without fighting for all of the females or brown people that are just like me. We are hopeful and ambitious and trying to leave our mark in the world. Wanting to be heard and taken seriously. Hoping to be treated equally against our counterparts.

I've heard about these situations, but I experienced it for myself firsthand.

Sometimes, when we think someone has done us wrong, perhaps they have done us a favor by making us do something we couldn't do on our own. A lot of times, we become comfortable because we play it safe. We are silenced by the fact that we need our job because we are all that we have. That's something society has taught us. We become reliant on our own strength and afraid to go where we are predestined or do what is right for all of us because we are afraid we will fail some of us.

Seasons end for a reason. My former employer thought they were closing a door on me, but they were holding the door open, so that I could walk into my future. I'm not walking in silent, because I confronted what wronged me RACISM/DISCRIMINATION! Maybe we need to understand that some things are a part of the plan. When things don't go according to your plans, think about the Our Father Prayer. God, let Your will be done in our lives on earth, as it is in heaven. God says that all things are working for our good and our latter days will be greater than our former days.

The sign on my mantle above my fireplace says, "BELIEVE." For years, there was something inside of me telling me that was just a dream. I kept telling myself to see beyond my circumstances and move forward, but life kept telling me everything that I believed in was only a dream. My reality was I had too many responsibilities to believe in my dreams. A lot of people define success by job titles, income, or even material things. How has anyone ever defined misery? That's what life became for me. Wondering if things would ever become fair.

For years, I struggled with depression and stressed myself out. I was in a dark place. I was undervalued and underappreciated. I remember days when I felt like giving up. Life was winning, and I was being dragged. There were mornings when I didn't want to get out of bed and face life. There were so many times when I sat in my car, trying to muster up the strength to walk into the building. There were nights when I didn't want to go home and face the people who were counting on me. I tried avoiding all phone calls from family and friends and didn't attend any events. I just wanted to suffer alone. I was accepting defeat. I'm being real. I was not ready to fight back.

This was a tough time in my life. There were prayers, but no answers; seeds, but no harvest; praise, but no breakthrough. It felt like my world was crumbling down. I kept shifting hoping I would find another solution. I went to dealership after dealership trying to find an opportunity. When I lost my job, life didn't stop, but my world was rocked. I prayed for an entire year for change, but it didn't show up the way that I was expecting it to. I wanted change, but maybe I was changed for someone else. Maybe I became the change that I wanted to see. I am not the only female or brown person that was mishandled.

Sometimes, our lives are rocked so that change could take place. Remember, everything has a purpose and some situations are just a test to help us grow, especially when God is teaching us something. I was praying for some time for change, but it came. To be honest, it never shows in suddenly without warning. It's always bad timing for me, but the right timing for God to rock the boat a little.

No one else can see what God is doing underneath the surface. Don't ever let anyone deter you from living your dream, be relentless, and let your voice be heard. Become the best you!

How to See Beyond
Your Current Situation

When we are able to see beyond ourselves, it means that we accept responsibility for every decision and action we make in our lives.

While driving, we are responsible for observing speed limits, stopping at stop signs, observing all traffic signals and signs, maintaining a safe distance between our vehicle and others, and any obstacles that may impede our vision or create the potential for tragedy.

Now, think about the wheel of life. The wheel of life has so many different things that allows you to navigate through life. When we are behind the wheel of life, as well, we must be mindful of every decision and interaction.

We are continuously confronted by circumstances where we do not have the freedom to choose, but we are still forced to consider. One of the greatest temptations in life is to become too absorbed in one's circumstances. There are many people whose vision is turned totally inward. These people can never see beyond their circumstances. What you want to do is try to imagine your life in a way that's greater than what you can see. I know this sounds easier said than done, but if nothing is too big for God, why do we worry about the small things of life? I will admit that there were times when I couldn't see how much bigger God was compared to my problems.

When I purchased my first home, I wasn't sure how things were going to work out. I wasn't sure if I would qualify. I made a very decent income, but I was covered in a lot of student loan debt. I had looked the year before but gave up because there were things hindering me. All I saw was negativity and some of the people around me weren't assuring me that it could be done, if I continued to work towards it. I decided that I would make more money the following year and then I would purchase my own home. I wasn't going to allow anyone to say what couldn't be done. There had to be a way around it.

When people get a raise, it could be anywhere from cents to a few dollars. It is possible to move into different roles and make more money as well. The following year, my income increased by $11,000. God will take us from one level to the next. I made some sacrifices, but I was determined I would see God move. I sold my car and caught a ride for six months. I needed to save money to clear off some of my debt. I didn't want anything hindering my house-buying process. It was chaotic; one of the toughest times I had ever endured. There were days when the enemy came against me. I was tired and frustrated. I will say this: you don't quit in the middle of the battle. Often, things won't appear to be what we think, but nothing goes unseen by God.

My loan processor vanished during the process. She had a lot of personal things going on and it got in the way. She just got sidetracked and dropped the ball. Doubt started to kick in for me.

One day in particular, I was off from work and just dwelling on my situation. I had talked with my realtor, and she assured me that I would be able to buy my house, but I was still feeling discouraged. I went downstairs to eat some peanut butter, and I heard God say, "The enemy has my permission, but you have my promise." Immediately, I thought of the Book of Job. Satan had God's permission to attack Job, but Job had God's promise. Job endured; he stood on God's Word and everything was restored. When I think of this, it reminds me how important it is to stand on God's promise during those tough times. Hebrews 11:1 says, "Now faith is the assurance of things hoped for, the conviction of things not seen."

At some point, almost everyone has found themselves in a Job like situation or perhaps feeling like Job. While going through hardship and times of suffering life can become overwhelming and we may want to throw ourselves a pity party. I have found myself questioning God asking why He has allowed certain things to come against me. Even when purchasing my home, things got rocky and I wanted to remind God of my effort and sacrifices. The book of Job documents the real anguish of a sufferer, discomforting questions, and alarming doubt. God's comforting words to me gave me hope as I relinquished fear that was trying to settle in.

Never give up because the greatest burden of life is to master the art of seeing beyond one's own circumstances. The ultimate test of life is how you respond to your circumstances. You can never change what happens, but only change your response to it.

Looking beyond our circumstances allows us to see reality as a whole, the bigger picture. Failure to acknowledge the bigger picture will make you look at the whole picture based off of a partial view. I found that every challenge that I endured over the course of life seemed huge in the moment, but when given time of reflection it was only a small picture of something greater.

The Encounter

Life will always bring unexpected trials and tribulations. However, there are good things that can come from life's encounters. As I moved further along on my journey of transitioning, I have connected with some great people who God has placed in my path. I truly believe that people are assigned to our lives. It is amazing when you think of how God aligned all of this before I even existed. I'm a small part of a big puzzle, but I'm a significant piece that adds value.

I can recall asking God if I could be just like Him. I wanted to have His qualities. I wanted to help people in some type of way. I wanted to be impactful globally. Have you ever just wanted something and once you realized what it took to get it you pause?

Sometimes, we want the gifts, we want the rewards, and the greatness but don't understand what has to be endured to obtain that level of greatness.

As I sat back and really gave thought about what I was asking for, at that very moment I came to the conclusion that leaders sacrifice for others. They put it all on the line. It's not about you looking good in the eyes of others. It is to help someone else. They are willing to put it on the line to clear a path or for someone else's benefit.

I once told my mentor, New York Times bestselling author, Omar Tyree, that I wanted to be just as good as my teacher. I look up to him. He is great at what he does, and I admire his work ethic. In the beginning, I saw all of his books, listened to all of his interviews and saw him as someone successful. I wanted to be a NY Times Bestseller as well. As the years went by, I started to see what it took for him to become who he is. I saw the sacrifices, the rejections, and him yelling until his voice was heard.

It has been an honor to work with him over the years and be able to call him friend. He opened his life up to me and allowed me to work alongside him, seeing the good and the bad firsthand.

Matthew 7:7 says, "Ask and it will be given to you; seek and you will find; knock and the door will be opened to you." I was never afraid to jump in and learn. I asked God to send the right people along and he did just that. We all want success, but no idea what it took. We all need someone that would believe in us and willing to share their knowledge.

All those years sitting in my bedroom, gazing out of the window and writing in my journal, I would have never imagined being passionate about sharing my story and helping others. Sitting in my college dorm room listening to motivational speeches and writing notes, I would have never imagined wanting to be an Influencer. Giving to others and helping people, I would never imagine wanting to sponsor a village.

I could have easily doubted myself thinking I could never have a mentor that is a bestselling author or even given an opportunity to learn from him. I didn't let fear stop me from asking for help or learning.

There is a plan for each one of us. There is significance in everything that we imagine. I was a kid writing in my journal about my feelings and here I am writing a book about those lessons I learned as a kid writing in my journal hoping I could help others see a greater picture. It was never even a dream that I would be in this very place.

I've always wanted to be a successful businessperson, maybe a founder of a company or CEO of a major corporation. When I started writing, I realized that I wanted to share my story and be transparent. I wanted to let people know that they weren't alone in their struggles because I felt alone for a very long time. This also allows me to show people that we can do anything.

I've met many celebrities in the entertainment industry that cheered me along as I pitched movies for Omar. I had no clue what I was doing, but I creatively wrote pitches that landed us interviews with BET, MTV, and Michael Elliot, the producer of Just Wright. I was on a webinar hosted by Michael Elliot, alongside my friends, Terrell and Dee. When I shared with Omar that I was on the webinar, he excitedly asked me to get in contact with Michael Elliot and set up an interview to discuss business ideas. I wasn't sure how I was going to set up the interview. I was thinking to myself, what? I asked God, "What should I do? What should I do, Lord?" How Am I going to make this happen?

Let's just stay here for a moment. I was on a webinar hosted by a famous writer just being a fly on a wall and listening and now I have a task to set up an interview. Why me? Why not me? I was chosen, but I think I needed to see myself. Remember I'm a small piece to a big puzzle.

This was a huge task that I didn't think I could complete. I didn't want to fail and look foolish or incapable. So, I kept saying Lord, I need your help. While utilizing some online sources, I found a contact for Michael Elliot's assistant, Allison, and then I sent out this comical email. I've learned over the years to be myself and what I do know is people like Twanja for who she is.

I told her that I was an assistant to Omar Tyree and told her a story about blind Bartimaeus when he heard Jesus was in town. The story of Blind Bartimaeus is about taking chances and not caring what others thought. He was creative and drew the attention of Jesus. Well, guess what? It captured Allison's attention because she emailed me back on a Friday night and I scheduled my first phone conference between Omar Tyree and Michael Elliot. I would have never seen my strength if I allowed my weakness to have control over my thoughts. In my nervousness I decided that I was going to take a risk. I came up with a funny and creative approach that made someone laugh and I was able to put together a phone call that some people may have never been able to do. There are so many people afraid to live their dreams due to fear. My advice to anyone looking to do something out of the norm would be step out of your comfort zone, become uncomfortable, and if it makes you nervous-DO IT.

The entire episode is an example of what happens when we turn the control of our lives over to God. It wasn't easy for me and I'm learning daily. As I continue to find myself, I realize my strengths and that makes life easier. So many things could have been different if I would have given up control and see myself differently. I can't change my past, but I can be better prepared as I move forward into my future.

There were so many more amazing doors that God opened for me. I remember when I pitched a screenplay to Brandon T. Jackson. I was assisting Omar with a screenplay and he wanted to cast him with a leading role. I went through a herd of managers, going around in circles. To my advantage, I had several friends in California with contacts that helped me. During this time, I had no money, but needed to access IMDb. I found out that you could have access to a lot of celebrities and their agents or managers on this website.

I became very resourceful and used free trials over and over with different email addresses to be able to access what I needed. There were several attempts to get the script over to Brandon and it wasn't working. His managers were not having it. I knew there had to be a way. I stayed up many nights surfing the internet. I finally found Brandon's email address and made contact with him. Then we linked up on social media. I was finally able to get the script that Omar wrote to Brandon.

I was thankful for the opportunity to network and step out of my comfort zone. I was able to assist on several other projects and thankfully found favor with many people. I contacted Ms. Debra Lee at BET. One contact led to another contact. There were so many people along the way. You know what else, I started every email letting people know that this was my first time assisting someone and how much this opportunity meant to me. They were cheering me on and wishing me the best of luck. There were A-List directors and employees from BET and MTV. The opportunity was huge, and this was a great learning experience for me. It showed me that I could do something that I never thought I could. It all started by me saying teach me what you know.

I had no clue what God had in store for me. I have so many more stories I could share. It was an amazing journey with God's favor. One door after another continued to open. When I started pitching for Omar, I had no clue what I was doing, but I didn't let that deter me from trying. Our journey is never in vain. The only choice I had was to become innovative and to do something different. I wanted to become creative and stand out from the rest. I also wanted to be impactful and leave a smile on people's faces.

If I would have never asked for an opportunity none of this would have existed. I used my gift of humor and creativity to push past my fear of not knowing.

Listening to the Voice of Direction

Listening to God is not always easy when we are distracted by voices coming from all directions. Just as in a conversation, you cannot hear the other person if you are talking or if your mind is distracted. When I pray to God for answers and I am waiting, I know that I must be quiet and sit still. It's hard to be still and wait when you feel a sense of urgency. You become like a toddler trying to capture the attention of an authoritarian because in that very moment your needs are important, and you need to express that. The stillness teaches us patience because things don't happen when we feel it should happen. There is always that waiting period. We spend so much time wondering when God is going to show up when in fact, He already solved the issue, we just needed to be still so that we could see that it was already worked out.

I've found that when I take a nap and wake up, I'm refreshed and that is when I find my answers. Answers can also come through people and signs as reminders. There are so many ways that God can speak to you. If you recall in the Book of Exodus 3, God spoke to Moses through a burning bush. There are no limitations on what God can do.

There was one morning I woke up at five o'clock a.m. and I decided to spend some time meditating. I knew this would be a good time to have my questions answered because everything was quiet. As I was meditating, I began to see something. The day before, my best friend and godson picked me up for a doctor's appointment. At that time, I didn't have a car and many of my friends would travel from different states to take me where I needed to go. I've learned that life doesn't stop because situations arise.

My best friend left work early, drove over an hour to pick me up, and then drove another hour to my doctor's office. My godson at the time was only a year old – precious, adorable, and very smart. Everywhere he ran, people would stop and say how cute he was. On our way out of the doctor's office, he was going in all different directions. His mom would call out, "Come this way" in a stern, but motherly voice. "Come on, you are going in the wrong direction" she continued until he followed her voice. He heard all of the other voices and eventually followed the right voice. This reminded me of sheep. When sheep's feel threatened, they huddle together and run away. The only way a shepherd can get a sheep to go where he wants is for him to gently lead it along, walking ahead of it.

At first, I was a little protective. I stood over him because I didn't want anything to happen to him. "He'll be fine," my friend told me. I backed up and just watched my godson. Toddlers can be self-assured, and they like to test you, but eventually they will listen. Just like the sheep, he knew his mom's voice and words.

This left me in awe because the Bible says, "The Lord is my shepherd," and I am referred to as "His sheep." A shepherd will search and search for any sheep that finds itself separated from the flock until He finds it. Jesus does likewise - He will pursue the lost people of the world, calling in a voice they recognize.

Staying Planted

Staying planted means to be set in soil for growth or being deeply rooted. "He is like a tree planted by streams of water that yields its fruit in its season, and its leaf does not wither. In all that he does, he prospers" (Psalms 1:3). Sometimes, we have to stay planted where God has placed us, even if it is for a season. God intended for us all to be successful at whatever we put our minds to do. When things don't look the way I think they should, I eagerly become antsy and convince myself that I am supposed to be doing something. The Word says, "Faith without work is dead." My mind is conditioned for me not to be still; I'm supposed to work. I'm always thinking, What can I do to speed this up? I often have to remind myself to know my season. There is a season of stillness, a season of working, a season of reaping.

Sometimes, we want to move when we feel things are beneath us, but God may have us planted in a spot for a reason. Many years ago, I was working at Target as seasonal help, and at that time, I had recurring back problems. I knew I couldn't give up. I had to remain planted. I couldn't let fear make decisions for me. I remember people telling me that I was only hurting myself more by pressing forward. People don't know what's best for you, only God does, and I had to learn that myself.

When we continue to ask God for His strength, that is what we will receive. I know the people around me back then were concerned for my wellbeing, but I believe we must speak to those mountains that stand before us. If I had moved out of the position, I would have missed a blessing. I had excruciating pain and I could barely hold myself up, but while I worked there, I met a manager from a well-known organization. She just so happened to be Christmas shopping on her lunch break. Since I have a habit of talking to people about anything under the sun, I started a conversation with her and found out her organization was hiring. What if I had allowed the enemy to move me from that place? What if I hadn't been planted? The job turned my situation around suddenly. A few days later, I sent that wonderful lady an email, and she connected me with the hiring manager of one of the other departments.

It wasn't a lot, but it was a notch up, and since I was just trying to bounce back, that move helped me a lot. Sometimes, we do not see it, but God puts us in places for a reason. We must stand still and be grateful. We could have short seasons to take care of something and wait until another door opens. All I knew in that moment was that my bills had to be paid somehow. I knew God would make a way, but I also had to put forth some effort.

The Plan

Having a plan is important because it is the foundation of helping us project objectives and achieve our goals. A plan can help define the scope of a project, but it also helps us to stay focused, set goals and objectives, meet deadlines, and measure success. Mapping out my plans says that I am intentional. Even though I have a plan for my life, it doesn't mean I've chosen the right direction. God's plan for our lives was predestined. Jeremiah 29:11-13 tells us that God knows the plan that He has for us. A plan to make us prosperous and not to harm us. God plans to give us hope and a future. Whenever we call on God and pray to Him, He will always be a part of the things we are doing. We have to invite Him in.

One of my favorite Christmas cartoons is Rudolph the Red-Nosed Reindeer. Rudolph, in my opinion, was a lot like David. He's hidden and overlooked because of his size and awkwardness. I understand the story is fictitious, but the story of Rudolph signifies a lot of what our lives look like today. Who doesn't want to be accepted and treated equally, to fit in with a group, or to feel a part of something? There are many people who long to fit in with the crowd, and never realized that God set us apart for a reason. A lot of people don't realize that just like Rudolph your difference could bring out your purpose. Your uniqueness tells a story that makes you necessary when in the right room. You may not feel accepted, but you are necessary to complete the task. We have to learn how to see our true story.

In Rudolph, there's a toymaker, Hermey, who wanted to be a dentist. Hermey knew he had a greater calling and wasn't content with just being a toymaker. He wanted to make sure that the toys had perfect teeth. None of the other toymakers understood Hermey's calling. As a matter of fact, Hermey was ridiculed and judged because he was brave enough to be different. He was determined to set himself apart and disciplined enough to keep going. He kept crafting his skill, like David in the Bible story, "David & Goliath." When the right time presented itself, his gift made room for him. His skills came in handy when it was time to take on the abominable snowman.

Hermey's situation made me realize that people may not understand the plan God has for your life. There will be times when people won't be able to see what God is doing through you. We should never give up because of what others think. It isn't their dream to understand. They are not the ones assigned to the calling.

Hermey was so determined, and he was willing to leave his toymaker life behind to live out his purpose. It's possible for people to discover their purpose while doing other things. Never base your dreams on whether or not others can see it or believe in it. Waiting on the approval of others could deter you from going after your dreams. I can still see the look on Hermey's face when he was ridiculed by his peers. Everyone laughed at him, and there will be people who will laugh at you too. People can make you doubt your gift, make you second guess your calling, and make you unsure about yourself.

In the end, hearts were turned when they realized the importance of Hermey's calling. Hermey went from being an outcast to saving lives. Hermey's fellow elves didn't understand his gift, but in the end, his gift elevated him in a way that he was able to save them. We should be mindful of how we treat others because they may just be our answer.

In Rudolph's case, his purpose was different because of his nose. The other reindeers treated him like he was a freak and didn't belong. It amazes me how this is a fictitious storyline, but in real life, people are ridiculed daily for being different. Once God was done, Rudolph was making history and changing lives.

You have to accept who you are in God's plan because you never know when your day to shine will come. God's plan will always come together.

The Journey of Life

No matter what a situation looks like, there is purpose in what you are doing. There is purpose in the journey of life.

You'll learn, as you get older, that rules are made to be broken. Be bold enough to live life on your terms, and never, ever apologize for it. Go against the grain, refuse to conform, take the road less traveled instead of the well-beaten path. Laugh in the face of adversity, and leap before you look. Take risks because you will never know what could happen unless you try. Dance as though everybody is watching. March to the beat of your own drummer. And stubbornly refuse to fit in. Life is always changing, so never be afraid to change or adjust with it. Sometimes, you are going to be up, but there will also be days when you are down. It's a part of the process. During those down moments, that's when growth takes place. That's where the work is. Never give up on your dreams just because of the time it will take to accomplish it. The time will pass anyway. Always remember that a new year is an opportunity to refine your purpose, and it is also an opportunity to redefine your life's vision. A new year is also an opportunity to bury the past and move into a new future.

My mama always said, "What doesn't kill you will make you stronger." Stronger is being able to withstand great force or pressure. Look at how far you have come from the point where you started. You want to look deep into your soul and realize that the person you are today couldn't exist if it weren't for the things that have happened in the past or for the people that you have met. Everything that happens in our life happens for a reason and sometimes, that means we must face heartaches to experience joy.

Take notes because on your journey, things won't always look the way you expect it to. You may start the business but don't see any fruit from it. Don't look at it, as where is my harvest, think of it as soon there will be a harvest and keep going. Never become sidetracked about what is next to come. Embrace every moment because there is something significant in every season. You have to pay close attention and become more aware.

In order to get something, you've never had, you must do something you've never done. Every time I decided to do something in confidence, I reminded myself of that. If I don't try, I won't ever fly. I want to be able to see how far I can go. The road will not always be smooth. In fact, through our travels, we will encounter many challenges. I found that I needed to stay focused, and I didn't listen to people who tried to tell me what to do. I listened to people who encouraged me to do what I believed was right for me.

Over the years, I have realized that when struggles occur, things begin to look up when I look up. Life is a journey filled with lessons, hardships, heartaches, joys, celebrations, and special moments that will ultimately lead us to our destination. Even though life happens, we must find the bright side in bad situations.

I remembered applying everywhere for a job in human resources. Diligently, I sent out emails because I kept telling myself I needed to make something happen. I could no longer afford to work part-time hours; I had responsibilities. My car engine had blown up around that time. I knew meeting that lady in Target was a part of the plan because of how everything happened. I knew that job would be mine and I had to figure out how to make it work. God showed me through a dream that two things were about to be manifested into my life. One of those things was that I was going to work for that company, so I already knew I had the job before it was given to me.

The night before my interview, I asked a friend to give me a ride and he agreed. I woke up early the next morning and prepared for my interview. I called my friend several times to see if he was up, but he never responded. I cried because I felt defeated. I asked God, what am I to do? I needed this job, and He already showed me that it was my job. "Do not be anxious about anything, but in everything, by prayer and petition, with thanksgiving, present your requests to God" (Philippians 4:6). I paced back and forth, asking God for a plan. I could have given up, but I didn't want to call it defeat. Faith is releasing from your hands what you already have and believing it will come back to you. What did I have that would get me to that interview?

I called the interviewer and tried to cancel. She said that she really needed to get this done today. I didn't want to lose my opportunity, so I asked her to move the time back one hour. She was fine with that, and I had a little more time to prepare. I called a cab and made it there for about twenty dollars one way. This was before Uber or Lyft. The cab driver was nice; he didn't charge me the full amount. The sacrifice was that I was using my rent money. This is what I could release from my hand so that it could come back to me in a different way. I've heard this old saying, if it can't fit the need it must be a seed.

The interview went very well. There were two women interviewing me and let's be frank, women like to share. It is a way that we bond. I shared how my morning was going, and one of them insisted on giving me a ride home. We can't give up when things shift, we will never know what will happen if we don't continue to move forward.

I believe God will bring forth the right people in your life at the appointed time to help you achieve your goals. This is one of those moments that reminded me that I promised to trust God. Continue to trust Him, no matter what it looks like.

Moments like this are the kinds of memories that show us that people are assigned to be in our lives. It amazes me how life is orchestrated. Just think about this, we are all a part of an assignment, and someone is waiting on us to do our part. It's hard to wrap my mind around someone waiting on me or something that I carry to move forward in their own lives.

Ms. Twanja Windley

There will always be challenges that will test our courage, our strength, our weaknesses and our faith. Along the way, we may even stumble across obstacles that will come between our paths that we are destined to take. In order for us to follow the right path in our lives, we must overcome the obstacles that come against us. Often, the obstacles are orchestrated to be blessings in disguise. We get so caught up in stumbling blocks, that we don't realize it at the time. There will be times when things won't go our way, but what's important is how we deal with life when that happens. Strength is found when you do something that you thought that you couldn't do. We must choose to find lessons in our circumstances because our struggles are developed by our strength.

Part II

Letting Go

Letting go is never easy. When you can let go, you are releasing power over your situation. Some people worry about their future; and some people live in their past, replaying those mistakes like their favorite song on repeat. No matter what you're holding onto, it makes it difficult to move on. Holding onto things keeps us from experiencing the joy of life, and we are unable to live in the present moment. If you want to change your mind, change your sound.

Are We Blocking God's Movement?

When I think of the word "movement," another word comes to mind: change. Be careful not to block what God is trying to manifest in you because you are afraid of change. Imagine being stretched like a slingshot so that your character could be developed. Slingshots are small weapons that could be used to shoot an object. Slingshots are stretched and just like sling shots we are often stretched in our daily activities. It's all a part of our growing stages. God could be stretching you to push forward your best ideas or stretching you in different seasons to make you become better. Stretching must take place so that you could land in the right place at the right time. Don't ever allow your past to dictate your future. Holding on to your past is believing that the past is the only thing that can exist. When you let go, it says you believe that something greater is ahead.

Many times, I held on to something that I needed to let go of, but I couldn't. I thought I was displaying my faith, showing that I was stronger, but the truth is my strength came from finally letting go. Letting go said I was willing to give up something for something greater. I've even found myself trying to dictate my outcome. This is an area that I find myself very guilty. I can't begin to tell you the amount of times I said, "Lord, let your will be done," but what I really meant was "Lord, let your will be done, but make sure it's what I want." I was always looking to do things my way when in fact, He knows what's best for me. Far too many times, I stood in the way of myself. I was a hindrance. When I finally let go of who I thought I was, and what I thought I wanted. I started to become who I was intended to be. The moment I let go of what I had, I received what I needed. Some things need to be released, so that God can release back to you what is needed.

Life may appear to be unexplainable or seem unreasonable from your perspective. It all comes down to the way you are looking at it. Life may even bring unnecessary pain, or loss, but the plan for our lives are so much greater than what we can imagine. It can be greater than anything we have to endure. These things are temporary. The Bible says "Weeping may endure for a night, but joy comes in the morning." Although it may include hurt and hardship, it always ends up being exactly what is needed to help us grow. No one is exempt, Life's unexpected moments are something we all may face at some point. Our journey in life isn't meant to be feared or planned, but to be travelled and enjoyed. Don't let the things that you see make you forget about the things God promised.

Strangely, we have the perception that the Christian life ought to be easy and free from trouble or suffering.

Consequently, if our expectations of a comfortable life are not met, we may try to change God's plan. But He's the One orchestrating whatever's going on in our lives. He alone knows what's required to make us into the people He wants us to be and exactly what will equip us to serve Him in the manner He's planned. Pain never means God doesn't love us. God is faithful.

I want to get more comfortable being uncomfortable. I want to become more confident being uncertain. I don't want to draw back because something is challenging, I want to push back and make more room in the area between "I can't" and "I can."

One night after work, I put on a video of Pastor Mike Todd at the Relentless Church while I exercised. The service was so powerful that I needed a recap. After my workout, I hopped online to listen to a business partner share her weight loss journey. She was having the conversation with some phenomenal women who were also eager to reach their goals. Then, I streamed a live video with Pastor Jamaal and Natasha Miller about how to prepare myself for" The One." Before I realized it, I had nodded off and woke up with a cramp in my hand. I was gripping my laptop so tightly and as I was getting up, a word was dropped into my spirit.

I thanked God for the process he was putting me through and reflecting on this very book. At the time, I was trying to finish it up. My mind started to trigger negative thoughts about how making changes would cause me to pay for editing again. I had erased the entire book and started over.

"Are you blocking God's movement?" I heard the Holy Spirit ask. I was shocked because here I was in my feelings and more concerned about myself. I was concerned about what it would cost me to change the message and less concerned about who the message needed to reach.

Hmmm. I was so focused on my vision and purpose of this book. I was upset about losing what I already put into the book and not what God wanted to do with it. I was also complaining about my time, effort, and resources. I was beating myself up because I invested a lot. I had to pause for a minute and remind myself that God would supply all resources needed to complete what He started. In the past, I've made so many things a priority and put in a lot of work with no complaints on the things I thought were making my life better. I'm guilty of working sixty plus hours a week chasing a life that made me miserable. And here I am complaining about small setbacks when I should have been honored to do this. Then, I started to change my thoughts. If God had brought me this far, I knew He would send provisions on how things would get done. Instead of focusing on the negative aspect of paying more money and putting in more time I should have reminded God who He is to me: Jehovah-Jireh, my provider and I trust that it would all work. Most importantly, I should have focused on how this book would become what someone else needed. I should have been more focused on how my words and thoughts would be encouragement to someone else.

Life can cause you to easily become distracted from seeing the bigger picture. It only takes a few minor issues to cause you to take your eyes off of the bigger picture and that is carrying out your purpose.

Allowing God to be your Pilot

An aircraft pilot or aviator is a person who controls the flight of an aircraft by operating its directional flight control. A pilot communicates with the passengers and crew during flights. The pilot also makes all final decisions about anything occurring during the flight. It sounds easier to trust a pilot, but why is it harder to allow God to have control of our lives? Being in control has always been a downfall for me because I've placed my trust into the wrong people or things and it failed me. I've had my guard up for so long, I didn't know what it meant to relax and trust God.

There were many times when I didn't allow God to be my pilot. I was afraid to give total control to Him. Sometimes, I was stuck on what I wanted Him to do and not what He wanted to do through me. Even as I write this, I realized that a part of living in purpose is to allow God to take me places that I could never imagine; open doors that I couldn't open, and to allow me to see a life that I couldn't imagine. There is so much that I have yet to discover in life. There is so much more learning and growing to do when I trust God. As my pilot, He knows how to get me where I need to be at the right time. When I decided to fully trust Him, I understood I needed to hand over complete control.

When a plane goes through turbulence, the pilot, who is more familiar with it, knows what precautions to take to get through the storm; but when passengers go through the storm, they begin to scramble for guidance and direction.

Turbulence is used to describe instability in the air around the plane caused by winds, air pressure, and other atmospheric conditions. I can recall times when my life faced turbulence. Things were shaken. Everything becomes unstable the moment things turn for the worse. During those times, I would allow God to be my pilot. I began trusting Him, knowing that He is fully capable of keeping me safe no matter what conditions I faced.

I remember during the time when I lost my job, I was trying to build my savings back up and I was devastated. I wasn't sure what would happen. I had so many responsibilities and I didn't have a plan because no one plans on losing their job. I was disappointed because I had recently spent a lot of money and my plan was to replenish what I had spent. I had to immediately take a timeout and I went to the sidelines to assess my situation. I couldn't understand what just happened. I had to stop and recognize my season. I had to acknowledge where I was at that very moment. I vowed that my struggling days were over, and I never wanted to see situations like these again, so again how did I get to this point. I felt like I needed a strategy because everything was riding on the line. Sometimes, familiar scenarios will replay in your head to steal your focus. I kept reminding God that I was here before and I remember what the outcome looked like.

I heard the spirit say, "You were once here, but I've expanded your thinking capacity since then,". "You aren't the same person when this happened before, so you have the advantage."

I had to continue to trust God and believe that things would turn out the way it was intended. Not knowing the outcome, that's easier said than done. The weight of life can hit you all at once and things can often become overwhelming. In that moment, I chose to believe that all my life God had been faithful, He has been so good, and I had to choose to know in this very moment He would continue to be faithful and bring me through what I was going through.

In basketball, when things aren't looking good for the team, the coach calls for a time out. This allows teams coaches to communicate with their players to determine a strategy or inspire morale, as well as to stop the game clock

The sideline helps you to figure out how to make smart decisions. Although regrouping to the sidelines sounds like a good thing, there are downfalls. The sideline also allows negative input from outsiders who aren't a part of the assignment. When I was in my early twenties, I would turn to people who couldn't help me to find a solution to my problems. I would end up leaving more fearful of an outcome than when I started. I've learned that that isn't always the best route because not everyone can offer sound advice. After falling on my face millions of times, I started hearing more clearly from the voice of my "inner me" about what was best for me. Becoming closer to God helped me to understand Him and His plans for my life. He became my pilot and the only person navigating me through my turbulence.

The Power of God

God Is A Healer, Not a Temporary Fixer

A few years back, I was going through the breakup of a relationship that I never should have been in. I've learned that you should never fight for a place in someone's life. No matter how hard you try to keep your spot, that person will put you where they want you to be, even if it's not where you feel you should be. This wasn't just an ordinary goodbye. My ex left me for someone else and then married her months later. It happens, and I paid a price for it. I was so angry at myself for allowing someone to break my spirit again and for allowing myself to believe that he cared about me. I felt foolish because I had made another bad choice. Yes, I said another. In my mind, Twanja was the person who had worked so hard to keep her life intact, who pushed so hard for success, but was terrible when it came to choosing the right guy.

It was like the breakup pushed back all the progress I had made. There I was again, wanting to suppress my feelings and bury them. After everything I'd manage to work through in counseling was I really about to allow myself to slip down that dark hole again. When things aren't talked about, negativity builds. Hurt can lead to being angry. I didn't want to grieve through my situation. I wanted God to take the pain away. I thought I was so strong that I could suppress the pain and pretend that he didn't hurt me. I cried every day and night for an entire year. The closer it got to my birthday, the more I didn't want to celebrate. I felt a heavy pain in my chest, and I wanted to hide from life. I'm not even sure what it was about my birthday that brought on the pain. I wanted to spend the entire day sleeping and wake up the day after. Instead of celebrating my life, I allowed depression, anxiety, and fear to steal that celebration from me, and steal away my new beginning.

Sometimes, simply getting through one day to the next takes an incredible amount of courage and strength. Nothing in life should ever have that type of hold or power over anyone, but it happens. In the process of letting go, you will lose many things from the past, but you will find yourself. If someone doesn't want to be in your life anymore, don't force it. Just let them go. God always has someone greater. You don't ever have to beg anyone to be a part of your life. Let go and let God do his job.

I used to spend every moment alone that year asking God, Why? I tried to convince myself that I was ok with what had happened and that my life wasn't over. The truth is I was not fine; I felt helpless. I couldn't make that pain go away, so I pleaded with God to take that pain away. Feelings of being buried alive don't die. I wanted God to alleviate the pain I was going through. I wanted to put all of it behind me and pretend that I didn't care. I tried so hard to believe that what happened couldn't break me, but I wasn't healed from the last time someone had stripped me down. I wasn't honest with myself or the situation. I allowed people to come into my life and take from me, but never once did I deposit anything back into myself. I was so used to sweeping things under the rug, but this one was huge. There was no space under my rug to hide it. This time, I had to clean up everything that I hid for many years.

Have you ever noticed that pain always occurs at the wrong time? You can never fully heal from pain if you don't dig deep to find the root of the situation. I found that patterns repeat themselves when you don't resolve the deeper issue. Once I started my path of healing, I discovered something. When I was growing up, our family was dysfunctional. I know, I get it, everyone has dysfunction in their family, but maybe that's the issue. Often, a lot of our problems stem from something connected to our families in the past.

Growing up, my siblings and I didn't have a voice. We couldn't talk things out or express ourselves. We weren't allowed to be angry, so I couldn't feel anger. No one trusted anyone and everything was confidential. I had no one to turn to as a confidant or friend in my own household. My family as a tradition swept things under the rug and pretended there were no issues.

Every day that we live in a painful environment, we start to feel like we deserve to be there. Pain happened to put us there, but we don't ever have to stay there. If we wait on people to apologize or acknowledge their part in a matter, it holds us captive. Adult-sized hurts are bigger because we carry around all of our hurt and add to it for years. Every day is a new day to forgive yourself. It's a new day to let go of your past, speak positive words into your life, and continue to move forward.

Although I didn't see it at the time, it was a process that I had to go through. God isn't a suppressant; He doesn't make things feel better for the moment. He is a Healer and He heals people from their brokenness. Situations will arise that aren't so pretty, but we must trust God to be who He said He is in our lives. We have to allow Him to show up how He said He would in our situation. Just because things don't seem to be working the way we expect it to, doesn't mean that God isn't working it out on our behalf.

My life is finally back on track, and I've discovered so much about me because I allowed God to heal me in a way that I've never felt. He taught me how to love myself and protect my space. That was probably the first time I ever had to protect my mental space from people. That situation taught me that self-love is the best love. You must learn to love yourself enough to get the help you need and not to allow anyone to disturb the gift that God has given you. Taking care of yourself is worth it. No one will love you like you do.

I know that healing doesn't happen overnight. It's an

ongoing process, but the biggest step for me was addressing the things that I hid from for a very long time. The next step was accepting things that I had no control over, and last, loving myself. I was always told that time heals all pain. I agree, but I also feel like time allows us to see pain through a different lens. Time allows us to find strength in our sorrow.

Trusting God

Don't ever be afraid to trust an unknown future to a known God. Trusting God means to rely on Him and place confidence in Him.

It's sad to say we live in a society where we only trust ourselves. My trust has to be earned; it is not given.

Like most people I have reached a point in my life that I've faced disappointment that has taught me to only rely on myself. Living for God causes us to unlearn what was taught to rely on ourselves. We have to find rest in God's understanding. Each day we should lay down our plans and expectations and surrender to His plans.

I remember the very first time I witnessed the power of God. When I was ten years old, I received a blue equinox radio for Christmas, but my parents forgot the batteries. I searched all over the house for batteries. I found two D batteries and one C battery. In my mom's room, there was a painting on the wall with an image of Jesus. I stood in front of the painting and touched it.

"Lord, please let these batteries work in my radio," I said to the painting. I stood there. believing that He could do it. I knew deep down that God could do all things, and He did it. This was my first miracle performed by God. This was my very own experience that kept me believing that God could do all things. It was such an exciting time. I remember thinking, God is real. I was in awe; I was overwhelmed with joy and an outburst of feelings. It was only the beginning of me trusting God. It was my very first miracle.

Everyone wants a miracle, but no one wants to be placed in a situation that requires a miracle. The only time we need a miracle is when we have problems and the bigger the problem, the bigger the miracle you would need. We like miracles, but not the problems that go with them.

I remember moving into a new apartment and the utility company wanted a deposit for my new place. I couldn't transfer my service over because a new bill was about to be released at my old place. The amount was astronomical, and I had a little over a week to pay it. To make matters worse, my new apartment wouldn't let me move in until the service was transferred. I tried to explain my situation to the lady at the utility company, but she wasn't hearing me. I grew frustrated, so I told them that I would call back at another time. Calling back at a better time was the greatest choice because I could tell my behavior was about to become obnoxious. I was working on my patience, but I had a hard time when people told me that nothing could be done – I still do. There is always a solution to a problem, and I won't let anyone tell me otherwise.

One thing that I have learned about myself over the years is that whenever I become frustrated, I need to leave it in God's hands and come back to it when I have a clearer mind and I'm out of my feelings. Whenever I need answers, I normally take a nap to clear my head. When I wake up, I am refreshed, and my mind is cleared. My thoughts become new. I knew I had to pay rent, get a U-Haul, and pay the utility deposit, but had no way of knowing how to get all of that done. That night, I went to bed, feeling worried and nervous. I knew I had to call Heaven to move some things around because that situation was beyond my control. I stayed up until early morning agonizing about my problems and talking to God. I surely didn't have enough money, but I was adamant that God would hear me. I slept peacefully after that, reassured that God would handle it.

The next morning, I called the utility company from the restroom at work. When I asked the representative if I could speak with a manager, she said, "Ma'am, can I help you with anything?"

"Ma'am, no disrespect, but I spoke to a representative yesterday, and she couldn't help me," I told the woman. "I need to speak to someone with some authority. I need someone who's going to move some things around for me." Sometimes, you just need to speak to the decision-maker.

She transferred me, but there was no answer. She came back and said, "Ma'am, I can leave a message for the manager to call you back." I gave her my number and a time to call. "Well, give me some type of idea of what this is regarding, so I can let her know." I explained my situation, and seven minutes later, the lady called back. I couldn't answer because I was in training at work.

Luckily, the lady from the utility company called me back with a blessing. "Ms. Windley," she said, "my boss said we can waive your deposit and you don't have to pay it."

See, I never gave her any attitude when we spoke, but I was firm in my request. Sometimes, you have to know how to state your desire with less emotion, so the other person can actually hear you. The Book of John 15:7 says, "If you abide in me, and my words abide in you, then come ask."

Now, that was the trusting God! The power of God will trump all things. It's those simple things that He does in our time of need. I like to believe that was a favor.

Sooner or later you will face something beyond your power or control. The next day, there was a waiting list at U-Haul, full until the following day. God always has a plan and a solution for all our problems. My best friend came from Atlanta to help me. I called another friend Fred to lend me his truck. We made several trips, and it only cost me $26 to fill up his tank. My friends and I had a great time. I got everything taken care of that day. God wants to face those challenges in our lives. Whenever situations occur, trust Him enough to know that He will provide for you in your time of need.

Sometimes small problems can appear so big and our

brain starts to opt us out of God's best for our lives. We somehow become overwhelmed with our situation till we forget the times God did the miracles in our lives.

I moved to be closer to work because of my transportation situation. The engine in my car had blown up and I didn't have the money to get a new one. God had this move mapped out. He had everything that I needed in place. When I went to view the apartment, the kind lady said to me, "If you pay the application fee within 24 hours, we will waive the $200 deposit, if you are approved." Plus, she said they had a special promotion that would give me $300 spread across six months.

This was exciting—to save $500. Once the lessor faxed over my lease agreement, my apartment turned out to be $11 cheaper than the quoted amount. Thank you, Jesus! That was $632 that I saved that year. There is something about the feeling of not knowing how things will work out but knowing God will work things out. When you are in a tough spot, everything that God does is miraculous. Everyone may not understand those little things that God does to change your situation. They don't know what you are going through or feeling at the time. I don't know about you, but when God does anything for me, I give Him all the glory and honor. I'm thankful. It's the simple things that He does. God won't allow you to see what is not there. Once you see it, that's a fact. The distance between what you see and where you are is called a plan.

Listening to God

We can believe in the miracles we see in other people's lives but won't believe God would do miracles in our own lives. One day, while reviewing my writing I asked God if there was anything I should share. I was more nervous about what people would think about my shortcomings.

I concluded that people would formulate their own opinions. Some may not agree with my decisions or choices, but I had to own them and do what I feel God is leading me to do. Faith believes God can do for me whatever I ask. I realized that every message isn't for everyone and that I can't continue to believe that people are going to get it, but the right people will.

We are all called for our own assignments. Following God, I've gained a level of confidence. I have become a little more courageous and fearless.

God has truly blessed me in a way that I never felt like I deserved. I could never do anything to earn it. There was nothing special that I could have done to receive God's blessing. My relationship with God hasn't always been the best, and I haven't always trusted Him. I've put other things before God many times. I wanted to do things my way and live life my way, but the older I get, the better I understand what's important.

I'm just trying to do what God wants me to do, and I'm honored that He would trust me to share my experiences. I have been working on many writing projects, off and on, for years. I would start over, give up, pick it back up, get frustrated, and quit over and over again. I allowed doubt to sneak in. I was worrying about something that I had no control over. Worrying was creating a negative illusion in my mind. If worrying can't change the past or the future it messes up today. We worry about a lot of things that are God's responsibility. Finally, I committed to finishing what I started when I asked God to help me clarify the vision for this book.

It seems like whenever we are doing what God calls us to do, we face obstacles that try to convince us to give up. We often won't be able to see where God is taking us, so it's easy for us to question our journey. I was struggling mentally and feeling unworthy to be a messenger. Can I be honest? Some days, I feel fit for the task and some days, I feel unworthy. Truthfully, many days I appeared to be put together well, but I was dying inside. A day couldn't go by without me crying out to God. I would ask, "Why do people treat me a certain way when I try to be good to them?" Worrying is assuming responsibility that God never intended for me to have. Every time I worry it's a warning light that I'm acting like God. I'm trusting me more than Him. You don't worry if you understand the goodness of God.

I remember the day when God told me that a part of me was hidden and not everyone could see my heart. That's just it, the right person will see it and be kind to it. I remember writing in a card to my former pastor: May God continue to use you. Then, it clicked in my head. I've been arguing for years about how I'm not going to be used by people anymore. It was never about me; it was about what I was carrying. It's about the gift.

Consider this: "I no longer call you servant, because a servant does not know his master's business. Instead, I have called you friend, for everything that I learned from my Father I have made known to you. You did not choose me, but I chose you to go and bear fruit, fruit that will last" (John 15:15-16). What if God is saying, "Even though people can't see who you are, I've called you to be you." Be you no matter what things look like or how people treat you. Through all the seeking I did, the tears and the praise, somewhere in that moment, I See me. I saw the person God created, the person who is set apart, the outsider looking in. My prayer was that iSee me, fierce as I am called, as iLead, as iLove, as iPray, as iDream, as iBelieve, as iShine, and as iServe. Once I started to believe in myself, I realized there is no need that God wouldn't meet if I trusted Him.

I needed to feel hopeful. There were many times when I followed God's Word, but that didn't stop me from becoming sidetracked. I was so concerned about how others saw me. There will be things you say and do that people won't always agree with, but as you travel your path, be focused on what God wants you to do. Don't worry about what others think; we all have our own journey.

Abide by what God is ministering to you. There may be times when you don't follow the message, but maybe it isn't your time to receive it. God may minister to one person, who tries to relay the message to you, but that may not be God's message to you at that time. It's important to understand your circumstances. God shows us different things at different times. You may not be ready to receive the message because you are not on the same level as that other person. I often struggled with recognizing when God was speaking to me. In prayer, the Holy Spirit instructed me, and many times, I allowed people to come in and bring thoughts to the Word that I received. I beat myself up because I clearly thought I understood what God wanted me to do. You have to follow God and, if need be, go back to prayer. Sometimes, while talking to God, I received confirmation to just be still. How can anyone be still when everything around them is moving rapidly, you might ask? There is so much that comes along with stillness. Being still allows you to do nothing and clear your mind.

"Be still and know that I am God" (Psalms 46:10). We live in a world of noise and chaos, but in stillness, we can hear God's voice.

LET YOUR LIGHT SHINE

I want my inside to be so bright that nothing can dim the light that shines from within me. May my light shine so bright that people would draw to me to be a part of that light.

The Bible says that we are the light of the world. A town built on a hill cannot be hidden. Neither do people light a lamp and put it under a bowl. Instead they put it on its stand, and it gives light to everyone in the house. In the same way, let your light shine before others, that they may see your good deeds and glorify your Father in heaven. (Matthew 5:14-16)

Sometimes shining requires finding forgiveness. We find forgiveness in light. Living in darkness only eats away at us because we want to be freed from it. Fear kept me paralyzed in darkness. I lived in fear that I would be hurt again by people who said they loved me. I felt unworthy and undeserving. I lost my self-worth and I hid in darkness. No matter how many people said they admired me, one person could say that I was nothing and that was all that I heard. I knew it wasn't the truth, but a repeated pattern of allowing the wrong people in my space said otherwise. There is an adage that says, "Sticks and stones may break your bones, but words can break your spirit." What does it mean to break a person's spirit? Someone's words once broke my spirit. I knew it was far from the truth, but they destroyed my self-esteem. I was left emotionally beaten to the point where I lost all hope.

People are going to knock you down and speak down to you, but when those things happen, you must somehow speak life into who you are. You have to stagger back up to find your balance. When people knock the wind out of you, stand strong. Constantly remind yourself of the good that is in you. Find your reason to fight. Be a light of hope. Find your strength in you. Dr. Anil Krih Sinha once said, "Let not others define you, make yourself strong and able to define yourself. When you accept yourself with your worthiness and weakness, you are invincible."

Don't compromise who you are to please other people. Settling differences by everyone making concessions is when we compromise. The one thing I've learned over the years is to never compromise my integrity by looking for outward approval. When being true to myself, the only approval I need will be from myself and God. I'm exceptional, gifted, and talented. I am unique and chosen.

Every person is unique. Each one is a complex blend of background, temperament, and giftedness. These differences, however, are often the root of unique relational conflict and pose all kinds of communication problems. So, simply put, we just don't understand each other. We may use the same words but have different perceptions.

I was born to dream. I was formed to be a visionary who will seek out the purpose for which I was created. No matter what may come against me, I was created to complete it with a spirit of excellence. It doesn't matter if people are for me or against me. It won't matter if people approve or disapprove of who I am or what I do. I am called to be here. My only concern is being pleasing to God. It is His will that I set out to do. I'm going to let my light shine; I'm going to be a source of strength and courage. I will share the wisdom that I've gained from falling.

Letting go allows you to lose things from your past and find yourself. How would you be different if you learned to let go of anger, ego, and that emotional roller coaster that keeps you going up and down? What about relationships that have plummeted? Old grudges, regrets, and all that could've and should've gone your way? What happens when you stop letting all of these things replay in their head? It's time that you free yourself from the burdens of a past that cannot change..

Understanding Anger - Let It Go

Anger can cause someone to be hostile. Hostility may cause you to become unfriendly towards someone, which means you're doing something to another person that causes them to react with unkindness or opposition. Anger can be a good thing, depending on how you perceive it. It can give you a way to express negative feelings. Anger can also motivate you to find a solution. It's all about the way you view it. You can determine your response or action towards anything. The power lies in you to determine your outcome. If you want to shed light on others, you have to glow yourself. It's time to start glowing. Let it GO!

Puffing Ego - Let Go

Sometimes, the ego can get in our way and allow us to put ourselves before others. When we get caught in our own ego, we can sometimes dismiss, minimize, invalidate, and ignore the feelings, thoughts, and experiences of others, especially our loved ones. We should never judge others because we have no idea what happened to them. Everyone has their own story. Who am I to judge the fruit that came up from seeds that were sown into someone? God is the only one who has seen all seasons.

Your inner light shines when you find peace within yourself and your surroundings. You must let go of the struggle you are feeling and seek your inner beauty. Allow everything to be and in the process be yourself.

Immense Emotions - Let Go

The constant focus on what's wrong with you will always blind you from seeing the things that are right with you. Let your inner light shine and others will begin to see the natural beauty that lies within you. There comes a time in our lives when we must release it all. Let your heart speak and let your tears flow. You need to get it all out. It's a part of the process, but it's never easy to do. Releasing our past hurt is the key to find healing; it's the only way to get there. You may even doubt whether it's right or wrong – that is ok. It's human nature to question yourself. It's the first step that you've taken, so you want to make sure you are making the right choice. I get that; I totally understand it. We won't ever know how things will turn out until it's completed. If you are seeking happiness, it's better to find it than just pretend. You don't ever have to settle. You will find that the struggle you are dealing with today will develop the strength that you will need tomorrow.

Feelings can be very confusing. I was always told to never decide things based on feelings and emotions. Feelings are powerful and can impact our thinking and choices. One of the hardest lessons in my life was letting go. I stayed stuck in situations for years, hoping something would change. The one thing that I learned about change is that it's never easy. We fight to hold on and we fight to let go.

God, Steer the Wheel

I don't know about you, but I have never had any success trying to boss someone around while simultaneously attempting to trust them. Trying to be in control and relinquishing control at the same time just doesn't work. These two things can't coexist inside the same heart. When we let God drive our lives and trust that He knows best, we can rest. We can cease striving and experience peace.

"Behold, I am with you and will keep you wherever you go and will bring you back to this land; for I will not leave you until I have done what I have spoken to you" (Genesis 28:15).

In the original Hebrew language, the phrase "cease striving" means "giving up by letting our hands down." If you want to experience the peace that comes from trust, you can't hold the steering wheel and let God drive at the same time. You have got to let your hands down; let go of the wheel.

When you trust and decide that you will let God drive, there is a natural rest that will occur. Imagine a woman who is trying to take the driver's wheel away from her husband. Now try imagining a woman who is sitting in the passenger's seat, allowing her significant other to drive without complaining, correcting, or cursing. It's nice to be able to sit back and put your trust in the one who's in control. I am enjoying the scenery. I am not fretting about how I am going to get where I need to go. I am just relaxing and resting, while enjoying the view. I enjoy looking out the window at my surroundings. Imagine how nice it would be to trust God in all that we do and know that we are in the right hands.

When we try to take the wheel away from God, it leads to emotional and spiritual fatigue. Why? Because we're doing something that we weren't created to do. God made us to lean on Him in dependence—to let Him drive. We were made to trust Him. That's why trusting Him brings us contentment. We become confident, knowing that we are exactly where we need to be, doing what we need to do, and fulfilling the role He created us for.

Have you ever noticed how difficult it is to effectively communicate with someone that you don't trust? When you try to take the wheel from God, it's a for-sure thing that you won't talk to Him the way you would if you had let Him drive.

When you're trying to steal the wheel from God, your communication with Him will be hindered. Words of gratitude will be replaced by complaining, and praise will be ruined by criticism. You will find that you can't communicate with God as easily because you'll think that He should be driving you better or somewhere else.

In the book, Reflections for Ragamuffins, Brennan Manning writes, "You will trust God only as much as you love Him." You will also only love God as much as you trust Him. As you drive along your journey in life, you'll find that confidence in God's love is always coupled with trust. As I said, this means letting Him drive. When love and trust are combined, they are like a match to faith. They will set your confidence on fire, so that you can ride anywhere that God is taking you without fear.

Letting God take the wheel can be hard, especially when life is tough and you're not sure where the road may lead. However, moment by moment, if you choose to let go and trust Him, you'll find peace, rest, contentment, communication, and love filling you up. You will also stay out of the emotional and spiritual ditch in your relationship with God. You'll get to sit in the passenger's seat and enjoy the journey that God is taking you on.

Letting go can be quite difficult for many people because they believe they always have to be in control. It's even more difficult when those people are not sure what they believe about God. If they have difficulty trusting another person, how can they trust a god they do not know exists or what he is like?

Even if we have a relationship with God and have positive feelings toward God, we still may struggle with our own self-will. Jesus said in order to follow Him, a person needs to lay down his or her own life. In some cases, this might mean becoming a martyr, but for most, it simply means surrendering to God's will in everything.

Someone once asked me if God was my steering wheel or my spare tire. How would you answer that?

Do you count on God only when things are bad, or do you rely on Him entirely? His promises have never changed: He will never leave nor forsake you. When we cry out to Him, He hears.

One night, I was getting into bed and heard some birds chirping. I wasn't sure if they were singing, giving praise to God or what. It seemed like they were on their own schedule and waited until night to start making noise. I hopped out of bed, so that I could see what they were doing.

"God, look at these birds," I said, staring out my window at them. "They're without a care in the world. Here I am getting ready for bed because I have to work in the morning. I have to work so that I can eat, and these birds are free. They don't have a worry or care in the world. They can roam around and easily find food." Then, Matthew 6:25-26 came to mind: "Therefore, I tell you, do not worry about your life, what you will eat or drink; or about your body, what you will wear. Is not life more than food, and the body more than clothes? Look at the birds of the air. They do not sow or reap or store away into barns – and yet our heavenly Father feeds them."

I am more valuable than those birds. I thought about my life and how much control I had given myself versus allowing God to have full control. I want to experience the joy of giving God total control over my life. I want to know what it's like to ask, and immediately, it's done. I want to be able to do God's will, knowing that all my needs are supplied without even thinking about it. I want to be able to live where my harvest is unlimited, blessings after blessings as I continue to sow. I understand that life comes with challenges, and often it gets hard before it becomes easier, but the promise is that there are better days ahead of me. I want to believe, as I continue my journey, that the seeds I have sown will manifest a harvest ahead of me. My future will be rich because of my seeds.

Psalms 46:1 says, "God is our refuge and strength, an ever-present help in trouble." A refuge is shelter from a pursuit of danger or trouble. This scripture is telling us that God is our safe place when we need protection. He is our haven. He is everything that we need.

Have you ever mapped out your life a certain way and expected God to make it happen the exact same way you thought He should? I have.

Life doesn't always go the way we expect it to, but maybe God is protecting us from ourselves. God didn't place me in any of the bad situations that happened to me; I did. God led me out of them, which wasn't easy. The insane part is that I've always prayed and prayed for change, but I never listened. I made my own bad choices.

I was so stuck on my own vision for my life that I wasn't listening to my prayer every night. I was saying it over and over all of my life but wasn't acting accordingly. Every night, I would say, "Lord, let your will be done in my life," but in reality, I was asking him to let me do what I wanted to do, even though he obviously knew what was best for me. He is the creator of my life. It is complete, but I wanted to take His place. I was praying that God would answer my prayers and not His plan.

When I began to let God lead, I found out that He was everything I needed. During a challenging time I heard the Holy Spirit say, God's peace will be like anesthesia in this season. It told me that I would walk through my situation and not feel a thing. God kept His promise and I walked through it like a brave soldier. Psalms 46:10 says, "Cease striving and know that I am God." That means to put my hands down and stop trying things my way. We're supposed to give up control of the wheel and let God do what He set out to do. By turning my life over to God, I'm saying, "Lord, I trust you." I can rest knowing that I'm safe. Everyone wants to let their guard down and feel safe, knowing that they can trust someone to be in charge over their life.

By letting God lead, I've discovered what rest is. There is a natural rest that takes place when we allow God to lead. Matthew 11:28-30 says, "Come to Me, all who are weary and burdened, and I will give you rest. Take My yoke upon you, and learn from me, for I am gentle and humble in heart; and you shall find rest for your souls. For my yoke is easy, and my load is light."

When taking the wheel from God, there is a feeling of unhappiness in my spirit. We all know when things are right and wrong. When we do things on our own, against the will of God, our spirit tends to let us know. It's called weariness because we are doing something we weren't created to do. The Book of Proverbs 3:5-6 says, "Trust in the Lord with all your heart, and lean not on your own understanding; In all your ways acknowledge Him, And He shall direct your paths."

By taking the wheel from God, am I saying I don't trust Him? Or is it that I prefer my own will over His? Isn't it hard to communicate with someone that you don't trust? Often, people tend to want others to see it their way or no way at all because they think they have it all together. Proverbs 18:2 says, "A fool takes no pleasure in understanding, but only in expressing his opinion." If you pay close attention when you are taking the wheel, you will find that you won't be able to communicate with God as easily. You'll be too busy trying to give Him your thoughts about how things should be done.

I've always prided myself in the way that I do anything. I get irritated when people try to challenge me and tell me how something should be. I'm thinking, I've been doing this for several years, and you can't come to me as an expert in five minutes. Show me where it is written. There's a role change when I try to tell God what to do when He is the author of my life story. It is written, and I don't need to question it.

Finding Your Strength

Sometimes, the only way to get people to move on is for something to push them. Many times, we don't grow unless we have to. I believe in myself. I know that God has prepared a prosperous life for me and He will finish what He started. I am worthy of good things. I am important, I am beautiful, and I am loved. This is what I remind myself daily. During my struggles, it was imperative that I spoke positive affirmations into my spirit. What I say about me is all that matters. With all the negativity that we absorb daily from watching tv, listening to the radio, or even social media, we must change the things that we feed our spirit. I had to change what I read, change the people I spent time with, and be mindful of the advice that I received from others. The hardest change is the change that happens within. It's easier to change your outer appearance with money, but the challenge is dealing with things that are internal.

Every battle starts in the mind. I know you've heard that little voice inside your head, trying to make you believe you aren't good enough and creating self-doubt. I was fighting a battle, and to be honest, there were times when I felt the weight of life. I wasn't sure if I was winning or losing. When you're losing, it can be hard to see the end of those times. I remember feeling like I couldn't pull myself together.

When I got fired from my job, my employer wrote some negative statements about me on my separation's paperwork. Immediately, I started to believe that I wasn't good enough. I questioned my work ethics and my abilities. Again, someone had spoken negative words over my life, and they weren't true. My value, however, doesn't decrease based on someone's inability to see my worth. If I wasn't already in the healing process, I would have allowed that moment to be another knock down. Not everyone that comes into your life will be for you, and we should never let the opinions of others validate who we are. We become stronger when we know who we are. When we care about what other people think, we will always be held hostage by their opinions and become prisoners to someone else's words. The late David Foster Wallace wrote, "The truth will set you free, but not until it is finished with you ."

I spent almost seven years in the automotive industry fighting for a fair opportunity, but the odds were against me. I didn't let this moment break me because I saw a possibility for change. Whenever I'm sad, I throw myself a pity party. When I'm angry and I've had enough, I'm willing to change. I decided to make myself a priority and not an option. Being fired can be hurtful and can ruin your reputation. I didn't want to fall back into a dark season. Immediately, I took control of my mind. I decided to pour into myself and started to imagine what I could become. The one thing I've learned is that it's never too late to start over.

I would stress myself out because I wanted everything to happen right away. I ignored the fact that everything happens in perfect timing. We must trust the timing of life. Everything is unfolding exactly as it should. Wherever you are on your journey, that's exactly where you need to be. Cultivating this belief or attitude will help you deal with whatever challenges come your way more effectively.

They say a new year is an opportunity to reestablish worthwhile goals. It is an opportunity to bury the past and move into a new future. If every day is a new beginning, then this was the beginning of a new year and new journey. I felt like losing my job was the perfect opportunity for me to redefine my purpose and redirect the vision for my life. You may feel lost and alone, but God knows that exact place you are in. He has a plan for your life to move forward. What's ahead is greater than what's behind us. He will show you the way.

Always remember the way you see yourself can change everything. Everything that has happened to you can be used for something good. The quality of your thinking is going to be the quality of your life. Your mind determines your direction, so watch what you feed it daily. When facing severe challenges, your mind is normally at its sharpest. Strength and growth come only through continuous effort and struggle. You are much stronger than you think. Sometimes, you don't know how strong you are until you have no other choice. There will be times when that strength has to come from within. I've found that when life happens, I have three choices: I can let it knock me down and define who I am or going to become. I can allow it to slap a label on me and my capabilities. Or I can fight like hell and let it strengthen me. You don't ever have to stay in a bad situation. You can create your own dreams. All the strength you need comes from within.

You can't be afraid of change. Sometimes, you may feel secure in the pond that you are in, but if you never venture out of it, you won't ever know that there is a larger body of water that exists. Holding onto something that is temporary may be good for now, but there may be a reason why you haven't received something better. You may not know what is going to happen when you try, but if you do not try, nothing will ever happen. Don't let anyone make decisions for your life. People may try to deter you or make you feel guilty for doing what's right. It's your life and you have one ticket. Live your best life, the way you want to live it. Change must come so that you can move forward. I'm honored that I'm able to share my story with others and I am praying that what I share brings healing.

Part III

The Changing of Seasons

People change just like seasons. Change allows you to
focus your energy on your future and to find a new
direction for your dreams..

Sowing Seeds

As I researched the term "sow," I found an acronym for the term which stood for "statement of work." I decided to dig a little deeper. I wanted to dissect the term a little further. A statement is something that is said or written, or a document declaration. Whenever I sow seeds, I am being bold and making a statement. I was always taught to name my seed and give it direction. We're supposed "to write the vision and make it plain" (Habakkuk 2:2). What am I sowing? What am I asking God to do with my seed? What am I asking God to do in my life? I continued to search and found an acronym for the term "work," which was defined as "worthwhile opportunities through resources and knowledge." Work means getting into motion.

The power of my seed is to work for me. When we plant seeds, we are expecting something specific to come from it. Whenever we sow seeds, the seed has a description. If I plant watermelon seeds, I expect my seed to produce watermelon. When I sow, I'm putting something into motion. My seed is created to bring worthwhile opportunities through resources and knowledge. My seed works to create an opportunity. And finally, "opportunity" is when something you desire is made possible. Once my seed is worked, in due season, a harvest is created. At the right time, my seed will bring forth a chance for something to happen. Just being able to understand the power of sowing a seed and knowing what it does on my behalf left me in awe. One of my favorite gospel songs is "It's Working" by William Murphy. Every time I'd sow a seed, I start singing, "I got seed in the ground."

We must plant seeds and wait on our harvest. There is something we need to know about our sowing and giving. Giving enlarges our capacity to receive. The harvest of one seed is always many times greater than the seed itself.

Think of the farmer. Every farmer has three intentions when he plants. First, he anticipates a harvest. Plowing and planting is difficult work and the farmer wants his labors rewarded. Second, he anticipates a specific type of harvest. If he wants corn, he plants corn seed; if he wants wheat, he plants wheat seed, etc. And third, he anticipates a specific size harvest. The magnitude of the harvest abounds in proportion to the amount of seed that's planted. In short, the key to farmers reaping their desired harvest depends on (1) planting, (2) planting a specific type seed, and (3) planting the correct measure of seed. There is one constant expectation at each of these three stages of farming: the farmer never stops believing that his labors will be rewarded. From the beginning, he anticipates a harvest.

Over 10 years ago, I heard a pastor share with us about tithe and offering. He said we should tithe on the level we want to be on. Sow into your future. That day was very memorable for me because it stuck with me. What I heard was in order to get something you have never had; you must do something you have never done. My pastor at that time, Ron Carpenter, always taught us that if we wanted to know if something was true, then test it. No harm done, right? God promised that His Word would never return to Him void. I had nothing to lose, but much to gain. I believed in those words, and from that moment, I started to sow seeds faithfully. There were times when I was down to my last, which was God's because I should have given it first. I had food for lunch, my bills were paid, but I didn't always have money to do anything extra. I wanted to know what that pastor meant about sacrificing and paying my tithes. I wanted to know what it would do in my life. Many times, my wallet would be empty, but I knew I had seed in the ground. I was saying to God that I trusted His Word and I was going to prove it to Him by doing what He asked.

Now, let me explain. There were good days and bad days, but my seed was going to create a future. All I wanted to believe is that better days were coming. Well, let's see it, God. Back then, I was in my mid-twenties, sowing into a Word that I believed, while expecting God to unlock the future that HE created for me.

Here I am, God, being obedient to Your word. I want to see, Lord; let me see. I'm hopeful, I have a believing heart. I know I'm not very good at trusting things or people because people have failed me, but I'm doing this. I want to see God. I trust this Word and I trust You. I know it's hard for a lot of people. I remember moving to a city, making minimum wage, even though I had two degrees. I knew I was going to survive because I had some seed in the ground. I knew I had this promise that God had made. I was sure everything would be alright eventually. I had overcome so many moments where I didn't have anything, but God stepped in. I understand the fear that people feel when it comes to sowing seeds. I was one of those people too. I didn't have much growing up, but I knew I wanted to have a better future. They say the greater the sacrifice, the greater the reward. I was willing to make sacrifices.

I started sowing seeds and trusting the promise of the Word. I saw the manifestation of it in my life. I found every bit of it to be true, and that was the beginning of my story. I also found that there were many ways to sow. If you sow okra seeds in the ground, you can expect to see okra when it comes time for the harvest. However, if you don't sow, you can't expect to reap.

If you sow bad seeds, you are going to reap bad seeds. People say Karma comes to visit. When I go through challenging trials, I sit back and ask myself, "What did I sow to reap such a bad turn of events?" Honestly, there have been times when I've said bad things about others, and I've been mean to people. I've snapped at people before, and when someone snaps at me or someone doesn't have patience, I always remind myself that I've had those moments too. A lot of times, I'm aware of what I've done and accept it as a bad seed. I'm also humble enough to know that God's grace is sufficient, and He loved me enough to get me through those bad harvest times. The Book of Galatians 6:7 says, "Do not be deceived, God is not marked; for whatever a man sows, that he will also reap. Everything that you sow will be reaped into your harvest

When we allow God's Word to produce good things in us, the results multiply. When farmers plant their seeds, they expect a harvest a great deal more than they sow. A single sprouted seed can yield dozens, scores, or even hundreds of seeds. When I was growing up, my mom would always plant a garden around a certain time of year. My mom would always say there was a season to sow. She had to get it done by a certain time to reap the first harvest, and if she missed it, she would wait for the next opportunity to get the next time frame. There were times when I heard my mom say that her crops produced more than she was expecting, and she always shared them with her siblings. Sowing seeds is never about the sower. It's about producing something that is going to help others.

There is a scripture that I always remember as I'm getting ready to sow. Whoever is generous to the poor lends to the Lord, and He repays him for his deed. (Proverbs 19:17)

I'm constantly asking God what I can do to help. I want to help meet the needs of the people that have less than me. I want my seeds to multiply and create a harvest that will be more than enough to change lives. I want to leave a legacy.

When God is the Source

My God is my source. He is who I depend on. He is my source of supply. He is the one I look to in times of trouble. He is my strength when I need help. He is a way maker. God is the water to my seed. I can't grow without him. Just like plants need water, I need God. He is my source.

I remember being short on my rent. I had an option of giving God His money by paying my tithes upfront or I could lift what I had to heaven and ask God to multiply my seeds. Well, I chose to trust in God. I was obedient in His Word and trusted in Him to provide what was needed like He promised. Regardless, I believed that things would work themselves out. That next day, I was conversing with a friend who was in a financial bind. He shared with me what his needs were. After our conversation, I went for my daily walk, so I could have some quality time with God. I spoke outwardly as if heaven had an ear. and asked God to move heaven now. When I returned home, I heard in my spirit to call my friend. I obeyed, but wondered what God was doing. A few hours ago, my friend's pockets were empty. When I called him back and explained what the Holy Spirit led me to do, my friend told me that he was blessed with a sizable check that day. He received a blessing in the mail. When we talked earlier, he hadn't checked his mailbox. He told me that he had just asked God what to do with the money, who He wanted him to bless, and God told him to sow a seed into me. I didn't even have to pay it back. My friend said to me, "Through your faith, I have built mine, and I want to sow this seed into you." When we release from our hands the thing that we are holding on to, God just may allow someone else to bless your situation.

You see what happens when we trust God and rely on Him, not our own understanding? We don't know how our testimony will affect someone else's life. We don't know how our prayers will turn someone around. For us to make it, we must encourage each other and be an example of God's Word. We should share our testimonies because there is power in messages. Someone may need to hear your story. I didn't always understand this, but I am beginning to scratch the surface a little. There is a reason for the season. I think that once we begin to transition our minds, we will begin to open ourselves up to seeing things from many perspectives.

Reflection can be a great thing when growth is involved. Reflection allowed me to understand that maybe I could look at things differently and hope to stumble across the beauty of situations. Reflection has also helped me reach forgiveness. There were so many times when I held a grudge because I didn't understand. What I went through was birthing my purpose. God was showing me who I was, but I looked at it in a negative light. I'm learning to just go through it and trust that I will see God's glory in situations. Some things won't always make sense now, but they're a part of life. Sometimes, I think I know how things will be or should work out in my life. That's how moments can be easily missed. In everything we do, there is purpose.

I used to cry everyday because I hated my job. I was so miserable and depressed. I cried out to God. Finally, I made peace with my assignment and respected it more. Once I moved forward, I realized the skills that I received from that position were what I needed for my next assignment. We never know why we are placed in a situation. I learned my strengths and the things that I was good at. I also started seeing myself as a different person with a new level of confidence. Some things, I think, can be avoided, but I believe God can shift us in the direction that we should be in.

Before I found peace with my job, I wanted a different position. I felt like the position I had was like starting at the bottom all over again. Truth is, we go from level to level. Whenever you are promoted, you are starting over from the bottom just on another level. I came to the realization that nothing I do is about me. It's all for a greater purpose, but I had to see beyond myself. I can't do anything without God, and I can't move until He says my assignment is up. Even when I feel like I've done all that I can, there may be more that God wants me to do.

I became humble and realized that the Word says, "We must be faithful in another's man work before God will give us our own." Here is the key: When we do for others, someone else will do it for us. While I'm playing a big role in someone else's organization, when it is my turn, someone will be working hard to help carry out the vision of my business. So, learn as much as you can, and one day, you will be as great as the person you are working for.

When I worked in management, I realized how amazing it was to work for two successful people who had created a debt-free organization. Now, you may think that sowing seeds is just putting in money, but this also includes your time and service. God won't forget about those things. You may not see the rewards now, but they are in place. I finally understood the concept that God is the rewarder of all things. He sees my effort. He knows what I do when people see me or when I am behind the scenes working. I do what I can at the capacity I am given and wait on God to move me to a greater capacity.

Growing up, my dad always asked me to babysit my youngest sister and brother. He always told me that I would be rewarded. When I looked to him the next day for my money, he never gave me anything. At one point, I started to believe he was playing me. I would never get paid. Little did I know, my work was never in vain. I stopped asking my dad for things because I thought he was being mean. I couldn't trust him or his words. When a person doesn't live up to their word to a child, distrust can happen. Even though my dad didn't keep his end of the bargain, God did. I think God was showing me early on about sowing seeds – the wait and then, the harvest, but I was too young to understand.

Now, as an adult, the seed has caught up with me. Be careful of how you perceive those tough lessons. Not only did my rewards catch me, but so did the principle. The blessings never stopped, and His words never left me. Still today, I receive favor from people I don't even know. It took a lot for me to realize this. I cried so much because of how I had been taken advantage of. I was so nice, my heart was so big, and people took me for granted. I even said I didn't want to be that way anymore. I came to the realization that God made me this way for a reason. I've decided to go back to the person that I used to be and accept that God was teaching me what it meant to sow seeds and reap a harvest. It didn't make sense to me then, but I surely do realize it now. Giving is a part of my gift.

We often talk about how life revolves. God's Word came back around for me. I'm still reaping a harvest from the seed my dad sowed into me. By telling me those simple words: "You will be rewarded," my dad had sown Kingdom principles into me. I never realized that I had the key to unlock everything I needed. It took time for that Word to manifest into my life. The seed was sown when I was a little girl, and in my thirties, I was still reaping the harvest from his words. Now, I understand what was truly meant by it.

I am sure there are a lot of people out there who are just like me, people who haven't fully understood that they carry a special gift. If they still haven't realized it. It is okay to go back and reflect. It is okay to be that person who loves to give again. It's never too late for change, especially when you know why. The best thing about change is that it's even better when you understand the reasons behind it. It's harder to do things when you don't understand the reason behind why you do them.

A lot of people are uncomfortable with change because as soon as they become comfortable, things may change again. Change means to alter, to transform, or to exchange for or be replaced by another you.

Change is bound to happen in everything that you do. If the competitor comes out with a new product that is better than yours, more innovative, wouldn't it be essential to modify your product and compete? Everything changes over a period of time. Nothing is like before. This is no different than the Word. When the Word cycles around again, there can be a new perspective. The Word doesn't change, but your understanding and wisdom does.

Who Are You Blessing?

When we focus on being a blessing, we are blessed abundantly. So, be the blessing that other people count on. The Bible says. "Give, and it will be given to you; a good measure, pressed down, and shaken together, and running over, will be poured into your lap. For with the measure you use, it will be measured to you." (Luke 6:38). I believe that when we sow, we position ourselves to reap increase. Giving is not about donating to someone, it's about making a difference in someone's life. The richest in the world are the people who give more than they take. Giving fills your life with things money can't buy.

When we give to someone, we should do it out of good cheer, knowing that we had an opportunity to help someone. I'm not sure if I'm the only person that struggles with this, but I sometimes have a problem with who I give to and this is opposite of what giving is supposed to be. As I think of it this may be an area in my life where I need some correction. There were times when I gave from a place of overflow and times when I gave from a place of lack. However, there were times when I gave from a place that was not cheerful.

I had to get my mind settled on the idea that

everything I have come from God. He allowed me to be able to do everything that I do. I try not to dwell on my current situation and think about myself. What I allowed myself to forget is that I wasn't always in a good place and I didn't always manage my money correctly. I shouldn't judge others' situations from what I see or hear. The only thing I can control is how I show up for someone in their time of need not why I showed up. My only position is to be a steward over what God has given me. He didn't call me to monitor anyone's situation. Looking at my behavior has allowed me to see myself in the mirror. Sometimes we think that we are doing right by giving, but if our hearts aren't right then what's the point of it. I was blessed with the opportunity to serve others, but I don't get to pick and choose who I serve or how I do it.

One day I was walking around my apartment complex and I saw an elderly lady with trash that needed to be taken out. "I don't mind taking it to the dumpster for you," I told her.

A week later, I was taking my trash out and I heard the Spirit say to me, "What you do for others, someone else will do for you." Seconds later, a guy pulled up while I was walking and told me to throw my trash on the back of his truck. He said he would take it out for me. I immediately started smiling because I heard God's promise to me.

Sometimes, I feel like we can miss out on blessings because we don't allow others to bless us.

I try not to take for granted because one day the things that we have may be no more. It could be the end of it. I would find a reason not to accept people helping me. On Earth, everything is in circulation. We have to keep things on the earth in constant flow. I blessed you and someone else will bless me. We must remember that God is our provider and all good things come from Him. If I'm blessing you, and someone is blessing me, and so on, the blessings will always keep coming. The widow of Zarephath is a perfect example of someone who stayed on the giving side of life, even when her resources had run out. She was down to her last meal when Elijah asked her to prepare a cake for him. When she did, she experienced an increase in her life. Not only did her resources multiply, but her son was also brought back to life (1 Kings 17:13)! A seed will definitely meet any need you have.

Can you imagine how many people have lost friends or family members because someone owed them money and didn't pay them back when they needed it? We've all probably faced this situation before. Can you imagine telling God, "You owe me money and I won't speak to you until you give me what's mine?" We may not realize at that time that whatever caused that person to not be unable to pay us back could just as easily have happened to us too. It could be a loss of a job, overwhelming bills, anything. We should love our neighbors and watch the way we treat them.

I remember lending a friend money and he couldn't

pay me back. I told him it was fine because I understood his situation. I saw him grind every day, but just wasn't making ends meet. He still reminds me that he will eventually pay me back. God told me, "Just because you bless someone doesn't mean that the person will automatically bless you. I am your provider and you are to trust in me."

Let's be honest. How many times do we rely on others to provide for us when we should look to God to supply our needs? It is His job to take care of us, so why would we rely on others? It's nice when people treat us or give things to us, but we can't rely on them to do that all the time. We must put our trust in the Creator.

It's hard not going back to people who you've done a lot for, because they owe us. We must remember that God is our provider. He is the reason we have what we have. If we need something, we should go to Him and try not to solve our own problems. We don't have to blame people or remind anyone of what we have done for them.

Keep in mind the power of words (Proverbs 18:21). Words are seeds. Whatever you speak will come back to you in the form of positive or negative manifestations. It's easy to become weary and give up when the pressure is on, but if you continue to speak positive, faith-filled words over your situation, you will see a breakthrough. Don't allow the devil to oppress you with the cares of life. God is faithful to pull you through!

You don't have to focus on your lack of resources

because you have access to Jesus's resources! Have confidence that He will provide your every need. John 14:27 says, "Peace I leave with you, my peace I give unto you: not as the world giveth, give I unto you. Let not your heart be troubled, neither let it be afraid."

Preparing for the Breakthrough

I assure you that the rain is going to come. If you stand in faith, God will deliver the breakthrough that you are waiting to receive. He will send a rainstorm of blessings. When the time is right, God will send an abundance of healing, of finances, of wisdom, of love, of protection, and of answers. You may not see the dark clouds arriving, you may not hear the wind whistle, and suddenly, without warning, God will keep His promise and your breakthrough will arrive.

Proverbs 6:6-11 says, "Take a lesson from the ants, you lazybones. Learn from their ways and be wise! Without supervision, a ruler to make them do work or a governor, ants will still gather food and labor hard. They won't have to be told how long to sleep or when to get up. Have you ever seen ants when they are on a mission? They are strategically moving in one direction like a product placed on an assembly line.

The ant is a prepping machine: no one must tell it to prepare for winter. It doesn't know how to do anything else.

We, on the other hand, were given a snooze button and comfy chairs. We must motivate ourselves because prepping isn't always easy. There will be times when you have to face those growing pains. It might mean giving up the things that made you comfortable so that you won't become comfortable and forget the real beauty of life.

How do you prepare when your season is about to change? I first try to identify what season I'm entering.

Everyone's situation is different. From my own experience, while waiting for my breakthrough, I try to control what I can and that is my mindset. I think about how I am assessing my situation. It's hard to stay focused on the outcome and not your situation, especially when your emotions get involved. The first break of a season we begin to visualize what we want our outcome to look like and we focus so much on proving to ourselves we got it. Meanwhile this isn't the season for that. I'm guilty of it. Have you ever felt you were fighting for something, but had no clue what you were fighting for? I remember hearing people say, you have to pick and choose your battle. What if everything wasn't a fight, but you created one in your head? I had to really think about this. Maybe I've created an illusion that I have a giant that I have to face, but what if I'm that giant.

I keep thinking about words to a song that say, who are you great mountain that you should not bow low, Jesus defeated the darkness and He never lost a battle. If the darkness was already defeated, am I going out looking for a fight? If I was given a promise of everything that is mine, then why am I believing it is on the way when it is already mine.

Your breakthrough is when you somehow get through that thing that is keeping you out or holding you back. God is the Lord of The Breakthrough.When God led the people out of Egypt, He led them through the desert and parted the red sea. For 400 years the Israelites were slaves in Egypt. The Israelites not only witnessed the power of God, but they experienced a breakthrough in their faith. After years of believing today would be the day and every time Pharaoh hardened his heart and went back on his promise. I couldn't imagine what they were thinking as they waited on God. It would be easy for anyone to lose faith looking at what was happening in their right now season. The story of Moses leading the Egyptians wasn't just a celebration of freedom, it was about renewing faith and a new level of trusting God.

The Israelites were free but couldn't become free because they could never change their mindset. I keep hearing this verse from Isaiah 55:11, so shall My word be that goes forth from my mouth; it shall not return to Me void, But it shall accomplish what I please, And it shall prosper in the thing for which I sent it. God kept telling Moses what to say to Pharaoh and here is what would happen. Pharaoh agreed, but then his heart would harden. If God promised the Israelites freedom and Pharaoh agreed, what took place that Pharaoh changed his mind. What if the Israelites' faith determined their next move? What if it was the mindset of the Israelites that kept them from moving forward.

God always responds to those who know what they want. The woman in the Book of Mark was determined to "touch the hem of the garment of Christ" so that she would be made whole (Mark 5:25). This lady knew that if she could get into his presence, something would break loose, something would change, and that she would find healing. Sometimes, you have to make those sacrifices to get what you have been waiting for.

Every day for months, I walked to and from work, about four miles roundtrip. I started off riding to work with some people, but I found myself needing space. I had nothing against others, but I was uncomfortable and just needed to be alone. My walk home from work became my opportunity to clear my head and enjoy my journey. With too many people in my face, my mind became polluted with other things. I would catch a cab to work and walk home in the evenings, but then I realized if I just walked going to work, I could pay off another bill. I came up with a plan to change my life and not focus on my situation. When we make a step, we can trust that God will guide us and help us fulfill our destiny. I was determined, and I didn't want to stop. In the evening, as the season changed, it grew hotter. Sometimes, I was so miserable from the sun that when I walked through the door, I immediately showered and passed out on the couch.

At one point, I thought, why do I deserve all of this? How much longer do I have to go through it? There were some very nice people in my path. As I walked home, people often honked their horns and waved to me. There were some people that I saw on a regular basis and they were cheerful. I saw this one lady driving a navy-blue Beetle. I remember seeing her every day.

One day, I said, "Lord, people who drive those cars appear to be so chipper."

As her blue Beetle approached me, the lady was waving like the kids on the show, Wonder Years. I thought it was the funniest thing ever. That made my day.

Take time and find humor in the little things so that you won't continue to view life as being hard. There is beauty in everything.

God has a way of putting a smile on my face. He will humor me along the way. There was a plus I gained from my circumstances: I began to lose some weight from walking. No matter what your situation may look like, you have to grab hold of what little greatness you can find in it.

I used to cut through a college parking lot, so I could bypass the traffic and walk alongside the road. At the end of the parking lot, there was a red 2002 Chrysler Town and Country van with a license plate that said, "Trust Him." I looked for that van every day. I would look up to the sky and say, "Lord, I trust you," especially on those days when I didn't think I could make it anymore. I would say, "Lord, I trust you," and it would give me an ounce of hope to keep going. I felt like it was a sign from God and that He was teaching me to trust Him because he knew that it is human nature to feel what I was going through. I was expecting Him to show up and help me figure out what I needed to do.

On my walk home, there were so many people who showed me love. People would stop to offer me a ride. One day, a taxi stopped and offered me a free ride. People would actually hold up traffic to offer me a ride. There was so much love. It showed me that no matter what we are going through, God will send someone to relieve some of our burdens. We were not made to do life alone, and the one thing that I've learned over the years is to show up for others the way that I would want others to show up for me. It may be your day today and my day tomorrow. Just don't outgrow your situation and look down on others when you move up.

It seemed like my habit of walking to work and home made me the topic of conversation around my job. I don't like any attention, but people made that hard for me. I realized that no matter what we do in life it will always interest someone. Just smile and pretend like they are your paparazzi's. There will always be someone in your business trying to get your story or create one for you. You don't owe anyone an answer or a story. People will always assume or make up something when they don't have answers.

When you talk less, it diffuses the energy around you. I had so much to be thankful for and with many years of trials, I knew I wanted more for myself.

When we are waiting on the breakthrough, there can

be so many discouraging things that may come against us. Discouragements will contradict what we are believing. It can take us off course and cause us to second guess our assignments or purpose.

The devil's greatest objective in his work is undermining and destroying my future (and yours) and causing worry. Worry is a negative flow of energy; it drains you. Worrying is the opposite of faith. If the devil can get you to grieve over yesterday, and worry about tomorrow, he has robbed you of today. Therefore, you must hold on to the promises of God and keep believing.

Things often appear to be ten times worse than they are when we can't see things clearly. If you strive to find the good in everything, it won't overwhelm you. There is nothing too large for God to fix. This is only a part of your journey.

We must believe that God can move those mountains that are blocking our path. The only way that you can win is if you win within. What are your thoughts about your situation? Are you remaining positive so that you could reach your destination?

"Thou shalt also decree a thing, and it shall be established unto thee: and the light shall shine upon thy ways" (Job 22:28). The power in your words is based on the strength of your faith behind it. I was convinced, all I needed to do was believe in myself and know that God would sustain me in order to pull through.

While at my desk one day, I felt the urge to write about my journey. I wanted to share how changing my mindset helped me see what God had given me. I journaled about my surroundings and how it made me feel. There were so many trinkets along my path. I noticed so many great things that the earth had to offer. I would have never seen the beauty of God's creation if I hadn't been walking to work. I saw blackberries and raspberries. I hadn't seen those since I was a kid, when my siblings and I used to sneak into the bushes to pick them while my mom was at work. There were many fruits growing on the trees and different flowers growing everywhere. I even noticed a park with beautiful flowers and the thought of a wedding came to my mind. I was far from marriage, but the idea was beautiful. It gave me hope for my future, a promise that God had given in Jeremiah 29:11, it felt like He was reminding me of that promise.

God promised to be on this journey with us and it felt like he never left my side. The Book of Matthew 6:26-27, says, "Look at the birds of the air; they do not sow or reap or store away in barns and yet your heavenly father feeds them. Are you not much more valuable than they are? Can you add a single hour to your life by worrying?" I certainly felt like God was saying to me in those hopeful moments that the goodness of the earth was still there and even though things appear to be chaotic there is still hope. The things of the past can appear to be negative or a reminder.

When things happened in my life, my brain would take off running and it made me unbalanced. I worried and became frightened just like the Israelites. I would pray constantly and never gave God a chance to answer, I was in panic mode. I would do all the talking and wouldn't listen. This was a period in my life when God slowed everything down for me. It helped me realize how anxious I was and how I never enjoyed anything that He gave me. I was always moving so fast and trying to hurry things up because I was afraid, He couldn't do what He said. At least that is what my actions were saying. It appears that my lack of faith created a giant (an enemy) in my head that I had to wrestle.

My aunt used to say that people are always in a hurry going nowhere. Worrying wouldn't move God any quicker. Sometimes, we want to fulfill the promise and skip over the process. We want the outcome without the journey. I am so guilty of that.

In God's timing, all things are possible. If God calls you to do something, He will provide everything that is needed to get it done. I learned that sometimes we need to go slow in order to grow.

T.D. Jakes said it best, "The real test of faith is in facing the silence of God placing you on hold." This silent coach takes your patience into strenuous calisthenics. Patience gets a workout when God's answer is no answer. However, don't fret. God's answer is not always yes or no. Sometimes, He says, "Not now."

As I Traveled My Journey

As I traveled my journey, along came a storm
As I traveled my journey, along came a storm
"Don't be afraid, I bring no harm."
I could hear the winds whistling, "Don't give up"
I fastened up my jacket; this storm was getting rough
The raindrops began to pour, beating up on me
Tears raced down my face
What do I owe thee?
I've done nothing wrong. . .
In the back of my mind, I thought, this storm doesn't know who I am.
 I am strong,
No matter how hard things get, I know I can make it.
Only one mile left to go till I make it to my house.
As I traveled my journey, I was so upset.
Along came a bird and I asked, "Are you chirping at me?"
"I came here to tell you to just cheer up," the bird responded.
"The storm comes and goes, so don't give up. I see this all the time, so hurry and finish up."
I had enough on my mind. "Why today?!" I yelled.

"Don't always think the worst," the bird said. "Just change your ways."

"Thanks, Mr. Bird," I said.

So, I changed the way I thought and started to scurry.

As I traveled on my journey, I noticed the trees.

The leaves were shaken, saying this storm is just a breeze.

I looked to my left and saw beautiful flowers blooming.

They said, "This is your gift for making it through this."

At the end of the street, I looked to the sky to see the sun peeking an eye.

It said, "I'm here to help you. See, you're almost dry.

"You haven't seen anything, so wipe the tears from your eyes!

"Don't worry, honey, it's only fear. God won't put anything on you that you can't bear."

"Thanks, Mr. Sun. Your words are cherished," I said.

Along came a rainbow and the rainbow said, "I am your promise.

"Hold onto your faith. This was only a test."

I smiled and thanked them for encouraging me.

I realized that great things happen in the midst of your misery.

One day, I was walking home from work and the rain was pouring down on my head. I heard God speak every step of the way. The moral behind this story is that even when the storm comes, so does the comforter. You can go through some tough times, but God will still bring you peace and joy. Don't miss the beauty of God, even when the storm comes.

Enjoy the things that God has given us and hold onto His pledges. He will never fail us. People often think bad things are from an enemy, but it could just be a period in your life where change is needed to break a cycle, to change your mindset and change your thinking. Some things happen in our lives to grow us.

The story I shared wasn't just make-believe. I really walked home in the rain one day, feeling discouraged. The closer I got to my home, the harder it began to rain. Then the moment I made it through the doors of my apartment, the rain stopped, the sun came out, and the birds started chirping. Earlier, a friend had offered me a ride that day. I said, "No, I CAN MAKE IT." It's like I had to prove that I could make it, no matter what came my way. I had to believe that I could do it by being tough. I knew that God was with me, and that I could do all things. When things happen in our lives, we must always remember that it won't kill you and this too shall pass.

As we wait on God, we can wait passively, or we can wait with great expectations. A passive person hopes that something good will happen and is willing to sit around, waiting to see if it does. The passive person is wishful. The person with expectancy is more like Blind Bartimaeus, who didn't wait for an opportunity, but created one. He couldn't see anything happening, but he believed he was closer to his dream. He knew something was about to happen. It was going down one way or another. The book of Mark tells the story of the blind beggar named Bartimaeus. Once Bartimaeus heard Jesus was coming, there was no stopping Him from getting Jesus attention. He didn't care what others thought and he didn't care what his past mistakes were. He saw an opportunity and was determined to take it. He thought it was his turn. No matter what his situation looked like, he believed he was next. He wasn't about to miss the biggest moment of his life. He had nothing to lose, but everything to gain. When you feel you've waited long enough, you start expecting something to happen. Your life can turn in seconds when you are positioned and ready.

When we wait, it means to remain where you are and be in readiness. This says, we are expecting and believing something is going to happen. Waiting can also mean "to serve," like a waiter or waitress might be called to wait on your table at a restaurant. I find this interesting, because in our wait on God as we are believing with expectancy, we could be serving and helping others until it's our turn.

Waiting doesn't necessarily mean to sit around passively, hoping that something will happen. We must be eagerly waiting in faith. Once we go to God for answers and to solve our problems, we must eagerly await His answer. I've struggled with that my entire life. We should serve with expectancy. Our waiting period can serve as a time of preparation for answers. Seasons are different, so it's hard to say how to handle them, but don't stop. Joyce Meyer posted: Stay full of hope and expectations, God's power is limitless, and He'll breakthrough for you. When we are waiting on our breakthrough, the wait allows God to work inwardly and outwardly in our lives. Psalms 27:14 says, "Wait on the Lord; be strong; and let your heart take courage, wait for the Lord."

Waiting is never easy, but it's always worth it. New days will bring new thoughts, new strength, and endless possibilities.

Nurturing Your Seed

Whatever you feed will grow. It is always your choice what grows. Either you worry or you're confident. Doubt or believe: the choice is up to you. In order to grow, you must nurture your seed, which means to care for it and encourage growth and development. Anyone, anywhere, can make a positive difference in your life. You have to be surrounded by things or people that inspire you to grow. A leader is like a shepherd. He stays behind the flock but allows the ready ones to lead. The others follow, not understanding that they are all being led from behind.

Think about planting a seed. We have to nurture the seed for growth. Imagine going back every day and digging it up to see if it's taken root. Sometimes, we expect more before the appointed time. We all have seeds that are planted within us. You may have a career change or a newfound talent and want to explore the reality of it. The moment you reach a point where nothing is happening, you begin to question if it was the right choice. The moment something begins to take too long, or the moment that obstacles occur, you want to give up or dig up your roots. Don't allow doubt and frustration to distract you from something that may change the trajectory of your future. Don't allow your seed to die because you uprooted it too early. Things take time to take root, germinate, and manifest. Just because you don't see something happening, doesn't mean it's not happening. Be patient, be nurturing, and be a steward to the seeds plantedz within you and watch it grow.

One day, I was conversing with my mentor about wisdom. I felt like I was supposed to get something from him but wondered what it was. He told me it was already inside of me; I just had to pull it out. Well, the next day, I was talking to my brother, Kevin, about the same topic. Out of nowhere, I found the answer that I was looking for. I truly believed that the answer was already inside of me. My mentor was right. As we continue to seek, the answers will come. Everything we need for our journey is already inside of us; we must search within for it.

With every new assignment, great ability develops and reveals itself increasingly. W-----hen you take on assignments, think, not of the negativity, but your purpose. There is a reason behind everything we do, and it makes things so much easier when we understand that reason.

Imagine being on a job you don't like and sitting there, beating yourself up because you feel out of place. I've been there and questioned why I was there.

I felt misplaced, I wasn't a good fit. A lot of times we accept jobs to take care of a need; we all need to pay our bills. Then shortly after settling in you realized that this wasn't your best decision. I have done this on many occasions. I allowed my emotions and circumstances to dictate my moves and ended up in places that didn't fit my calling.

I kept in mind that God wouldn't steer me in the wrong direction. Something greater was ahead. Eventually, it all came together. Think about this: gardeners have to nurture their crops and that requires a great quality of patience. They have to always be persistent.

Even when you take those pitstop in life and you feel like you've made the wrong turn, you will still learn something along the way that will take you into the bigger assignment. Nothing goes unused.

I wanted to work for an international company and one day, become a CEO. That was a great idea, but not what God had for me. I've had days that had me crying on the stairway because I was so miserable. I was unhappy because my plan wasn't working. I wanted more for me; I really didn't know what that was at that time because my plan wasn't coming together. I wanted to bypass the process and go straight to the top. I had potential and that is how I justified it. Finally, I accepted the place that I was in and took it for what it was. I wasn't going to give up.

If you nurture your mind, body, and spirit, your season will eventually expand. You will gain a new insight that will allow you to gain so much more. The Bible tells us to "be anxious for nothing."

I realized I could only move when God said it was

time. I tried hard to believe that my assignment was up, but it wasn't. I saw myself doing greater things, but it appeared out of reach. Why couldn't I be an Apple Executive or the CEO of Amazon? Even though Apple or Amazon wasn't a part of my plan, I still think of the places where God led me on my journey.

I managed a Waffle House at age twenty-three. I worked in automotive sales and made a good living, and then I was a finance manager in the same industry. One day, I will become the face of my own company.

What if my path in business was cultivating me to become a business owner? What if God allowed my desire to keep stirring so that I wouldn't lose focus? What if all those seeds I planted building someone else's dream was to teach me what it took to start my own business?

After 23 years of learning different aspects of business from people of many different backgrounds and ethnicities, I have solidified my mark in the business world as a real estate agent. Everything I've learned over the past 23 years will allow me to build something for myself.

There could be multiple reasons why God may place you somewhere. Instead of being in a hurry, like I was, take notes of the journey and allow God to be in control. I often remind myself that this is not about me and I'm thankful that He saw fit to allow me to be here.

Working in sales, I felt like I deserved more and wondered why I had to struggle. There were months when I went home disappointed and I had to remind myself that God was in control of things. If He wanted it to be different, He would change my situation. Those situations were learning points. When I worked in automotive sales, I had to stand in the heat, waiting for a customer to show up.

It was hard, but I learned a lot from those experiences. I had to work on the skills and patience it takes to deal with the public and those who weren't instant buyers. By crafting my skills, I was preparing for a brighter future. I had to learn not to focus on the hardships, but to focus on the destination. Nothing in life is easy, but just remember it is a part of the setup. We can easily become discouraged when the plan doesn't look the way we envisioned it. I came to realize that the problems we face are so small compared to the God we serve. little problems, BIG GOD. Tell yourself this as a reminder when you start feeling bogged down with issues. Know that God is bigger than any problem that may arise.

It's possible to enter a person's life and be a blessing or a reflection. It's also possible to be absorbed by their negativity and forget what your purpose is. Look at it this way, "The purpose of life is a life of purpose" (Robert Byrne). There is a reason for which something is done, created, or exists. Observe things to its smallest details. You have to break things down, ask lots of questions, and find answers.

There was a time when I couldn't understand why I was at the bottom again. I had worked so hard to get ahead, but I was reminded that I wasn't at the bottom; it was a part of the process at a new level.

In every position, you will always start at the bottom. It's a new beginning, but on a different level. You may work your way up to the top, get a promotion, and then start at a lower level in your new position. In life, we are always students, so we should be teachable. As soon as I learn as much as I can, I will only advance to start learning from someone else.

It doesn't matter how many times you start over; it won't be the same. Life changes and the atmosphere will shift, but you won't ever be at the same place you started. Growth is continuous. It is a stepping stone to many achievements. There will always be change if you are looking to see something different. At times, it won't be measurable, but if you pull hard enough, it will be noticeable.

The past is gone, and I don't want to relive those days. However, the memories are still there. I'm so thankful that God allows us to put our past behind us, forgiven us, and has given us grace to move on from it.

The moment we live in our past is the very moment that we should leave it behind us. To forget about your past isn't something that comes easy. It is going to take a lot of effort, time, patience, and self-respect to keep pressing forward.

I surely don't want to jump through all those obstacles again. Living in your past allows old doors to stay open and new doors to remain shut. If you can't truly let go of what's already done, you won't allow yourself to have a better present or future. The reality of life is that we only get one chance at living it.

Growth requires us to change and change requires taking a risk. This means that I have to allow myself to step from the known to the unknown. Growth is impossible without change. You have to be willing to change in order to grow. Without changing your mind, you cannot change your life. If there is one thing I've learned is to always try to maintain a positive attitude no matter what I'm going through. I call that another level of thinking!

There were times when I was very scared, but I had to remind myself that today won't be anything like yesterday and that I have no control over tomorrow. I can only have faith and believe in my future. Faith is about not knowing how it will happen but believing it will. The only choice I have is to start where I am, use what I have, and do what I can. I trust that God will do His part.

Here is a little advice: you can't get yesterday back once it's gone, so don't be afraid to move forward. I can never go back to who I was yesterday because I'm a different person today. However, I can learn from my past as I continue to move forward into my future.

There will be things that will try to hold you back or make you lose confidence in yourself. Hold onto the vision and the promise that God has given you.

Life is short, so enjoy your happiness. Our past doesn't define us. You have the ability to decide who you want to be in this life, and you have one opportunity to live it. True happiness resides within. If you allow your past to take control over your thoughts and your life, you won't ever experience true happiness where you are in life currently. Faith and strength are necessary to live your happiest life.

I remind myself that I'm good enough daily because for quite some time I heard the opposite of that in my head; There will be times when things won't work out, but that isn't about you or your ability it may not be your season.

I heard "No" many times when I was trying to get bookstores to purchase my book. I started to feel weary. Nevertheless, I told myself that God had prepared this day for me and that everything was in order. I refuse to let rejection get to me. Rejection only forces me to work harder. God would finish what He started. Rejection is a hard emotion to deal with because no one wants to hear no.

No matter how many times you tell yourself that there is a yes coming, soon you are going to wonder when. Rejection is a hit to our ego that makes us question ourselves, it can also trigger insecurities. These are perfect moments to remind yourself of who you are. Your season will come. When we plant seeds, the harvest must come. It has to because the bible says, "While the earth remains, seedtime and harvest, cold and heat, winter and summer, and day and night shall not cease." (Genesis 8:22)

I remain confident that God will help change situations. Rejection is what makes you stronger; it is the push to keep going. Something may not work out the first time around, but that doesn't give you a pass to give up. It gives you an opportunity to fight harder. You must fight hard to reach your dreams, make sacrifices, and work hard for it. If it came easily, there would be a possibility that you wouldn't learn anything from it. You may even bypass the purpose in your experience. There is only so much of a situation that we can see, but God sees the things we can't see. When we are rejected, God may be protecting us from a season he didn't intend for us to walk in.

A strong woman has faith that she is strong enough for her journey, but a woman of strength has faith that in her journey she will become strong.

I've never wanted to be the person to drag everyone with me. People tend to become offended when others walk out of their lives. Has it ever occurred to you, that you weren't meant to walk in seasons with others? I am sure you've heard, "God won't place more on you than you can handle", but a lot of times we try to walk into seasons with others that weren't designed for our lives. Sometimes, we just need to sit things out and cheer people on from the sideline. You can't go everywhere with others when God has a specific plan for you.

It's imperative that you know your season and what God is saying to you in that moment. Be mindful of who you let speak into your life and what they are saying. I had to learn that there will always be confirmation. Be sure you aren't hearing what you want to hear and that you are hearing what God is speaking. Trust that God has a plan for your life that is already written. Understanding that He has a plan in place makes it easier to swallow those hard pills of rejection.

My former pastor said that "diligence is when you keep doing the little things until something big happens." Diligence is all about waiting while expecting, knowing that it will happen. Don't let the little things discourage you. Just keep doing whatever it takes until what you want happens.

I've always said I wanted to be Oprah Winfrey's successor. I have a heart to give, but I knew I couldn't give on that level with the capacity I was working with. So, I do what I can. I give on the level that I have. I keep reminding myself that God knows, He sees, and He is able. I may not reach millions of people right now, but I can reach a small number with my limited resources. I never felt like I needed to be rich in order to give. I don't have sponsors, but I will always give what I have from my heart. Someday, I will receive sponsorship and I will think about how I was diligent in my giving. It doesn't matter what I have. God will give seed to the sower and allow me to keep sowing.

It doesn't happen overnight, but everything starts

with movement. So many people started from believing that they could. Even when it didn't look like they would be able to do it, they kept pressing towards it.

One of the greatest basketball players of all times, Michael Jordan, was crafting his skill and doing what people said he couldn't. He did those little things and God opened many doors for him. God sees our effort, our passion, and our desire. You don't have to wait to become anything. You can be anything right now. I think a better expression is "Waiting while expecting." It makes more sense and sounds better.

Learn from the Things We Face

Back in college, there were two cousins in my English class. On the first day, our professor asked us to tell who we were and a little bit about ourselves. The cousins shared that they were cousins and the first in their family to attend college. Both young men shared their struggles and how their grandmother wanted them to become more than what their circumstances dictated.

I remember this day because both young men had said they weren't sure how long they would be in college. It was a struggle not having money and they felt like they should have found jobs then went to college.

That semester, those young men were using other people's meal plans every day to eat. I would see them at the laundromat on campus, washing their clothes together to save money. It was tough for me, but I had the support of my family. I had started seeing the fruits from the seeds that I had sown growing up.

Before the semester ended, both guys had dropped out because it was too hard for them to survive. They didn't know how to make ends meet. I've seen it happen so many times. This inspired me. Witnessing the struggle that those two cousins faced, along with others, made me want to become an answer for others. I believe God wants me to start the Twindle Foundation Scholarship Fund.

I've acquired so much debt from going to school, but I want to help others who are willing to step out on faith and meet them halfway. I want to be able to help people live their dreams, despite their circumstances. Sometimes, if someone knows another person is rooting for them, they may push a little further. I don't want money to be an issue for anyone to get an education. There are a lot of children who are raised by their grandparents because of circumstances, just like those two guys. All their grandma was trying to do was see to it that her grandkids became better men and had better opportunities. She wanted them to have more than she could give them. I want to be the answer to the prayer of those grandmothers, believing that their grandchildren can have a better life.

When I was in college, there were people waiting to help me through my tough times. In my junior year, I didn't have a computer and needed one. I saw that the computer lab in the Business Building was upgrading to new computers. I went to my business professor, Professor Yates, and asked what they were doing with them. He told me he'd find out. When I got the call from him, he told me to pull up at Media building, at a certain time, and he'd meet me there. When I arrived, he told me to pop my trunk. The school had apparently decided to give me a computer. It wasn't new, but it got me through college.

Ms. Twanja Windley

I give as much as I can to help people pay college tuition because I know what that is like. I know soon the Twindle Foundation will be launching and I will be able to provide financial relief to thousands of people. This will help alleviate the burden of tuition, so that college students can focus more on learning and less on debt. When I was in college, I wished I was a lot more focused on school, instead of worrying about making ends meet. I want to give others an opportunity to break cycles in their lives. When we fight and push for what we believe in, we'll be surprised by what we can accomplish.

I used to sell jewelry for extra cash. One weekend, I decided to go to the flea market to make some extra money. When I got there, I noticed that there were a lot of people there hustling. The customers were mostly Hispanics and they were looking for a bargain. All the vendors were selling for a low price, and I couldn't compete. I could not afford to drop my price as low as they did because I wasn't purchasing from the same market. I packed up and threw in the towel.

At first, I was a little discouraged because I spent twelve dollars renting a booth and I only had fifteen dollars to begin with. I walked around, looking to see what my competitors were doing differently. I wasn't going to quit forever, just to come up with a different plan, or maybe even move my business elsewhere. I have always had a passion for business. I like to get my head in the game. You can learn from anyone. I started talking to some of the other vendors and I received the answers I was looking for. In the beginning, my thoughts were to rent a booth to make some money, but God had a different purpose for me. I was sowing a seed to gain knowledge, and the reality is I didn't walk away empty handed. The knowledge I walked away with had more value. I went in looking to make a profit, but I walked away with the kind of knowledge that was going to make me more for my future.

Knowledge is power. Knowledge can be a passport to your future. Tomorrow belongs to those who prepare for it. Sometimes, you are sent for other reasons. Be open minded so that you can gain in every situation. Don't let your frustration overtake you to the point that you are unable to hear or see what God is trying to show you.

This experience was very significant to me. I was strongly considering expanding my jewelry business. I am the type of woman who seeks until she finds. I've always liked trying new things. If I'm led by God, I can't go wrong.

In both situations, I saw myself building a foundation and I have always known that I would be an entrepreneur. It's been in my heart since I was six years old. Every opportunity has been a chance to plant seeds for my future. There will always be a reason why you meet people. It could be to change your life, or maybe you will be the one to change theirs. Starting a new business can be scary, especially because most businesses don't make it beyond five years. Those who succeed in life are the ones that have failed but keep failing until they finally get it right. I failed on my first day of selling jewelry, but I took home knowledge that I could use for my next business venture. I don't regret any of the things that I've done. I regret the things I didn't do when I had the chance.

Part IV

The Finished Product

Everyone wants the finished product, but no one wants to go through the process. Give your gifts time to develop and submit to your assignment. Persist under the pressure. The pressure of life tests the reality of your gifts. Pressure is important for the seed.

It's Time: Stepping Out in Faith

Maybe like me, you love the idea of an adventure, but going through it frightens your inside and takes you out of your comfort zone. That is exactly how I feel when I'm stepping out on faith. Like most people I get nervous thinking about the unknown- immediately I start to think about those what ifs.

One thing for sure, you can expect God to act when you step out in faith. I've always believed in living my dreams, but there were times when I relied on timing to make moves. I would convince myself that I needed to get this done or that done before I could make any type of changes.

That was a part of my control issues. I had to see things a little clear before I could take action.

I think a lot of it had to do with the fear of sinking and not me being in control of my own life. When I focused more on the outcome instead of the source, that produced fear. I know God said to do this so it doesn't matter how it will get done. It's already done because He has called me to do it no matter what it takes.

At some point in our lives we are all faced with stepping out of our comfort zone. A part of our seasons changing is so that we can grow in Christ and depend on

Him. When we step out on faith, we won't have all the answers. We have to be willing to go when God asks us to.

Stepping out in faith can help restore your mind and change your outlook. The renewing of your mindset will allow you to see things from a different perspective and also help to keep you out of your head with bad thoughts. There were many times, I found myself regurgitating old memories of what happened in my past. It was a familiar spirit and I was stuck trying to make my past situation my current situation. I was becoming stuck and I was wasting my energy.

It became beneficial when I retrained my thoughts and focused on how powerful stepping out in faith is instead of shrinking in fear.

To accomplish great things, we have to not only act, but also dream; not only plan, but also believe. The challenges didn't stop, they were just beginning. Every time I took two steps forward, I had to take five steps back. When we step out in faith, it forces us to depend on God in a way that we wouldn't otherwise. This was definitely a test of my faith. There were days when I cried and wanted to give up. I was exhausted, mentally and physically. I held onto God's promises. His promises are greater than anything of this world. The world can't stop anything God has set in motion. Having faith is worthless without the faithfulness to see it through.

Sometimes, there are events that happen in our lives,

that we can't control. The only thing we can control is our response to the things that happen. Your response to something will always determine what you will receive from that event. Sometimes, the manifestation you have been waiting for will hang on a thread, just barely unseen, waiting to see if you believe the Word more than what you see. The manifestation is waiting to see what your response will be.

WHEN YOU CHANGE YOUR RESPONSE, YOU CHANGE THE OUTCOME

You cannot respond in fear to any event. Fear paralyzes you. Fear generates its own outcomes. Every event deserves a response, but you can choose how to respond. A step of faith means that you understand that God gives us enough information to see in front of us and releases the information as we move forward along our journey. Sometimes we must look at hardships on our journey as an opportunity to step out in faith. We get to exercise our faith by believing and trusting God like never before.

When I settled down and allowed faith to take over, I became overwhelmed with joy seeing God working through my situations. There were so many adjustments that I had to make with my workout routine and work schedule it all became taxing.

In faith, we have to give everything to God to do His will. In faith I relinquish my plans for His plans and all the uneasiness that comes along with it because I know He will always have my best interest. "Surely goodness and mercy shall follow me all the days of my life ..." (Psalm 23:6).

With everything I've gained over the years, I was finally able to see myself in a different way. I was starting to become everything that I stated without fear. I felt like things started clicking in my head. The moment you change your mindset will be the moment you can transition into that place you desire.

Personal Development

Personal development is a conscious choice to improve my life, to become a better person, and to grow as an individual. As life goes on, I realize that I can step forward and grow, or I can step backwards into my safety net. Personal development is a lifelong process. It is a way to assess your skills and qualities. It allows you to set reasonable goals in order to realize and maximize your potential. Every day, I listen to personal development because it helps to strengthen my core. When I hear the word, "Core," I think of the middle of a fruit or stabilizing my core when I'm working out. Core is defined as the central or most important part of something. The core is the tough central part of various fruits, containing the seed. Personal development strengthens my core, which allows me to protect the seeds that I'm carrying in my core until it is time to birth them. It's like carrying a baby for nine months and preparing for that right season. Once you are clear on where you want to be, you can start planning how you are going to get there. "But seek first his kingdom and his righteousness, and all these things will be given to you as well" (Matthew 6:33).

When you connect to your core, you will find strength, but when you act from your core, you will move mountains. If you are uncomfortable leaving your comfort zone, then you probably haven't left it. Whatever struggle I face today gives me the strength to overcome what comes next.

When I focused on personal development, I saw things that helped shape me. I focused more on observing people. I became more aware of my surroundings and the people in my surroundings. People were hurting and I could relate to the hurting pain. I remember carrying pain bottled within and no one ever noticed. From that bottled pain, I discovered empathy for others.

Empathy is understanding what another person is feeling or going through. It is seeing the world through another set of eyes. Our trials allow us to relate to others. I won't smother the fire and pretend like it didn't happen. I try to live my life transparently, so others know they are not alone in the fight. You can relate to or understand a person when you feel them in yourself. Often, we tend to become judges of each other because we don't understand. I believe that we are supposed to serve others, show compassion, and to help others. We can't do life alone; we need each other.

Personal development has given me a new level of confidence. For a very long time, I held my head down and wished that I wasn't seen. I pretended that I was invisible, but I wondered why I felt like no one saw me. I was overlooked and undervalued, but I became assured once I saw myself in the image I was created. You may not know this, but even when you are broken, God will heal those broken places. Your self-esteem and your self-confidence is basically what you think about yourself. Confidence and success go hand in hand.

Personal development taught me that it is of the utmost importance to spend time with me. I had to learn that it's mandatory to spend time in my own space and do things that I love to do. Solitude can be quite healthy. There are many physical and psychological benefits to spending time alone. Solitude allows you to reboot your mind and unwind. Whenever I'm constantly thinking, it doesn't give my brain a chance to rest and replenish. Being alone allows me to find peace with no distractions. It's an opportunity for me to revitalize my mind and body at the same time. Solitude gives us an opportunity to discover who we are and find our own voice. It provides time for us to think deeply. Clear the voices of others from our heads. Solitude gives me an opportunity to discover myself and find my own voice. When we're a part of a group, we're more likely to go along with what the group is doing or thinking. These aren't always the actions you would take or the decisions you would make if you were on your own. When you spend time alone, you can learn your own voice, engaging in deep thought and formulating your own opinions. It's hard to think of solutions to your own problem when we are always looking for others to solve them.

Don't ever feel guilty for making time for yourself. It can be a challenge to find some time alone, especially when you are everything to everyone. I get it. I've lived that life for quite some time. My excuse was that I needed to help this person and that person, and work was my priority. One day, I found myself miserable, broken, and depressed. That's when I realized that I was my number one priority, and change was vital.

Personal development helped me figure out that letting go of my past freed me. One of the biggest hindrances to personal growth is holding onto the past. For me, finding my joy is imperative to stay out of the past and live in the present. Strive to become more mindful. It's benefitting to acknowledge the abundance that already exists and is a part of our lives. Instead of constantly replaying your past, which no longer serves your interest, or worrying about a future that you have no idea how it is going to be, we must learn to live in the present and enjoy every moment.

I worked on growing my mindset and making better decisions. When your mindset changes, the way you perceive things begins to change. You begin to see things from all angles. I incorporated a habit to make better decisions. Our choices determine the life that we live, and our decisions help shape our lives. At a young age, I picked up that my attitude defined who I was as a person and my attitude was poor. Having a great attitude helps achieve what we want from life. A positive mental attitude can move mountains. Happiness begins within. Your happiness depends on your mindset and attitude.

Self-Discipline

I was long overdue and had to make a choice. There are two types of pain: the pain of discipline or the pain of regret. I had to decide which pain I was willing to endure. Self-discipline is when I have the ability to control my feelings and overcome my weaknesses. It's the ability to pursue what I think is right, despite temptations to abandon it. Self-discipline is a key ingredient to my success. I can't achieve any goal without using self-discipline. It allows me to control impulsive urges, emotions that will have me bouncing off the wall, crazy desires, and unusual behavior. Somedays, I can be up and feel like I am in all control, then the next day, I may be down and feeling unsure about all the decisions I've made.

In order to gain self-discipline, I had to be able to make decisions, take actions, and execute my plans, regardless of what obstacles, discomfort, or difficulties that would come. No matter what the obstacles or challenges looked like, I kept going and did it anyway. You don't get to quit because it is hard, uncomfortable, or you have a need. Those things will always be around, it won't ever leave.

When I wanted to start my weight loss journey, it took me an entire year to say yes to myself. I wasn't sure how I was going to make it happen. My life wasn't in order, but I had to adapt and make changes to living a healthier lifestyle. I have been taking high blood pressure pills since middle school and I'm already in my late thirties. It was time I gave my heart a break. It's worked hard for me the first half of my life. I was determined to live a longer life, so I needed to discipline myself now. Being disciplined does not mean living a limited or restrictive lifestyle. In fact, it taught me how to make better choices. I didn't give up the things I loved completely; I've just taught myself that I needed to be disciplined. Also, I can love healthier things as much as I love unhealthy things. Creating a healthier version of the things that are not so healthy made a big difference. There are always ways around things when you want to change. There are no shortcuts when you are trying to reach your goals.

Being self-disciplined gave me the confidence that I never had. I found the ability to do what I needed, even when I didn't want to. On days when I wanted to give up, I remembered why I started and empowered myself to push forward. In order to make my dreams a reality, I knew it would take an awful lot of determination, dedication, self-discipline, and effort. I can never just wish for it; I have to work for it.

I also learned that the more disciplined I became, the easier my life started to become. Self-discipline and willpower can lead you to the road of success. Willpower is the inner strength that enables you to refuse indulging in unnecessary and useless habits. It is inner power that enables you to overcome inner and external resistance and obstacles. Self-discipline is the ability to reject immediate satisfaction, pleasure, or comfort in order to gain something better. Whenever we have strong willpower and develop self-discipline, we can overcome negative habits. Accomplishing my weight loss goal gave me the confidence I was looking for. I felt empowered and inspired to take control of other areas in my life. I was able to see myself in a different way, like this new me could accomplish more. It's powerful when you can see yourself in your own power.

I've never felt so accomplished. I can maintain a higher tolerance for frustration, obstacles, and negative emotions. A negative thinker sees a difficulty in every opportunity. However, a positive thinker sees an opportunity in every difficulty. The journey has allowed me to walk with peace. My daily walk with Christ provides peace and purpose. Having God's peace has allowed me to trust Him in a way that I've never done before. Living a life of peace is more than the value of a dollar. After working for years, trying to secure the bag, I realized that the only thing I'm looking to secure is my peace. We should live our lives in a way that allows us to incorporate peace in our daily walk.

Coming from a family of five, peace never existed. I moved away for college to separate myself from all the family drama. It's hard not to get sucked back in. One day, I figured out if I was going to live a life of peace, I would have to work for it. Obtaining a life of peace meant I would have to set boundaries. Every day, I have an opportunity to choose. Am I going to allow people to offend me? Am I going to let them invade my space? Will I easily get upset or worried when life happens? People will always get on my nerves; family is always going to be family and that won't ever change; and unexpected bills will always present themselves. Life will always happen. If I waited for things to calm down in order to have peace, I would have never found it. When you train your mind to receive life as it is, you'll receive peace. It's how you reckon how life is with how you want it to be.

No one is exempt from difficult times nor did God say that storms wouldn't arise. However, the promise is that He will give us peace during the storm. God promised to give us peace that surpasses all understanding. Despite what is going on or your circumstances, you will have peace. I didn't get the promotion, and the other person was less qualified. I wasn't treated equally compared to other employees. I was paid less because I'm a female. It's hard to turn the cheek and allow people to walk all over you. The Word says, "Cast your cares on the Lord." The moment I realized that God was in full control, that He would be the vindicator, I was able to walk in peace, knowing that He would make things right. It wasn't an easy fight because I had to trust that God would stay true to His promise, even as my character was defamed.

During that time, I had to learn that sometimes, we don't understand what people are dealing with, and that the same grace we ask God to give us is the same grace we should give others. At times, it's difficult, but we aren't perfect; neither is anyone else. I heard Pastor Mike Todd say, "What happened to you isn't a punishment; it's a platform for God's glory to be seen."

In order to maintain your peace when life happens, you want to shift your focus. Don't get sidetracked by the little things that come your way. Sometimes, things are hard to let go because we keep focusing on it. Focus on forgetting the past.

Be grateful, it's over. Whenever we complain, we are focusing on the things that frustrate us. When we allow our focal point to be on all the negative things that occur, we are overlooking the positive. This takes us away from our peace. If you want more peace, stop getting into this vicious cycle of dwelling and complaining.

You have to cut down the negative sources to keep your peace. I prefer to surround myself with friends who encourage me, instead of the ones who panic and cause me to worry. I've learned from experience that not everyone knows how to cover me. A lot of times, we want to solve problems with our flesh when we should speak God's Word over the situation. Speaking God's Word brings peace. When facing something negative, you have to cut it off from the root and not allow it to disrupt your peace.

To keep your peace, you must take care of your mind and body. The body achieves what the mind believes. It is our duty to keep our body in good health. Otherwise, we won't be able to keep our mind strong and clear. Schedule a set amount of time daily with yourself to read a book, focus on your thoughts, think of minor goals you want to accomplish, workout 30mins a day, or recall a time that made you happy. Find your happiness and don't let anyone rob your peace.

To keep your peace, you should remove extra clutter. Do you spend a lot of time on social media? I do because I have a business and I use it as a promotion tool. I have to be honest; I prefer not to be on social media. Social media can become draining. Often, I have to log out for weeks, or even months at a time. One of the reasons why we can feel so drained is because we focus our attention on too many things. I'm very observant and I tend to read a lot of sad stories. By the time I'm done, I am emotionally drained. Focus on what is occupying your space, time, and thoughts. If your space is over capacity. It's time to declutter your box and empty your storage.

For years, I allowed a conglomerate of things to take my happiness, peace, and energy. My life became a masterpiece when I learned to master peace. Once I accepted that releasing was God's desire, I decided to focus on change. Change is required and doable. Never underestimate your power to change yourself.

Seasons

"To everything there is a season, and a time to every purpose under the heavens" (Ecclesiastes 3:1).

Seasons ends, situations change, friendships fade, but God alone remains the same yesterday, tomorrow, and today.

When I was growing up, I remember knowing exactly when the season would change. Like clockwork, we knew exactly what to expect, but as the years progressed, things started to change. It was as if the seasons were out of whack. Everything became unpredictable. Just recently, I was waiting on God to shift the season of my life because I was looking forward to something great. The season never changed. I felt like I was going through the motions, wondering daily when the season was going to shift. It was extremely hot during the month of October and we were already in the fall season, but the weather was still in summer. I could feel a shift on the horizon of my life, but everything was moving too slowly.

God will lead and guide us through each season of our lives. Each season gives us an opportunity to embrace change, to let go of something, and allow change to take place. "He changes times and seasons; He removes Kings and sets up Kings; He gives wisdom to the wise and knowledge to those who have understanding" (Daniel 2:21). I knew that everything operated on God's time, but this time, I understood that nothing moves until God moves it. It doesn't matter when man thinks it is supposed to happen because He is the creator of all things. This shows that it is our job to keep sowing seed and wait with expectancy for the harvest, but wait, I say, on the Lord.

I changed. I was no longer holding myself hostage to my past, pains, and wounds. I was no longer feeling captive in my childhood, wondering why things happened as they did. I could feel free knowing that little girl who was hurt by bad choices could finally be herself. I was finally able to see my life from a different perspective. I finally put that inner kid in her place, so that I could grow. I saw my past for what it was; there were no more excuses. It was time to see beyond it, so that my season could change. Every story of my life was used by God as a stepping stone to bring me to where I am today. I had to stop thinking that I would be stuck in a situation forever. There were times when I felt my heart would never heal or it was impossible for my struggles to end. Don't confuse a season for a lifetime. Even your trials have an expiration date.

Life isn't peachy or perfect. I accepted that I won't always enjoy the taste of life, but as I grow older, I have begun to understand, to change, and to accept those bittersweet days, which allow me to change. I have started appreciating life on a different level.

There were many things I had to learn in order to reach a level of change. When I did, a season in my life shifted and I began to blossom. Changing my mindset took work. Formed habits aren't easy to break, especially since many of my most harmful habits and counter-mindsets were established when I was a kid. I kept looking at it from a one-sided perspective.

I had to discover who I was created to be to reach this place of transition and change. Change helped me walk into a new season of harvest. I was created to be happy; even when my circumstances said differently. I was brought into this world to experience the greatest joys that life has to offer and nothing less.

I finally discovered what letting go was about and what was waiting for me once I truly let go. Trusting fully in God is an ongoing learning process. Just know that God knows we won't ever be perfect, and He doesn't expect us to be. "God you know me, and I trust You with my life," Tasha Cobbs Leonard sings in her song, "You Know My Name." I love to sing this song when I'm going through change. I rewind that verse repeatedly and say those words to myself over and over to help me come to terms with God as the author and finisher of my life. Who would know me better than Him? No matter what I was up against, I could rest assured that wherever and whatever God took me through, I wasn't going in alone. I knew that wherever He led me, it was key for what was ahead of me.

New discovery has brought a new season of change for me and everyone who is attached to me. I can't be anything for anyone else if I'm not whole for myself. I've learned what I've sown is what I reap. If I continue to work on myself, I can always expect a better version of me. I work out daily, when I initially started it was about losing weight. As I progressed, I started seeing a change in my perspective; my mind was clear. As I took my healthy lifestyle to the next level, I started to see a greater progression. I became more disciplined, my endurance increased, and for the first time in my life, my mind was sharpened. I felt a covering of peace. I started to imagine a greater future and visualize myself doing more. I started to believe my dreams were possible, I felt them coming to life.

I look forward to the next phase of my life. I've reached a place of healing, I've learned the importance of self-love, trusting the process of life, and *allowing God all access. I feel whole and complete.*

Completion

There is no way you can be complete on the outside when you are broken on the inside. Living a complete life is an ongoing process. Life is about evolving into the complete person you were intended to be. My mental state is so important to me, and I focus daily on having a sound mind. Every day, I take steps to become a healthier me. There was so much I had to learn about myself. I thought I knew who I was and why I did things a certain way, but I didn't.

Letting go has always been hard for me because it felt like I was abandoning someone who needed me. The truth is I was abandoning myself. I taught myself to hold on tight to things that I should have let go of and justified it as me having faith that it would work. I wanted to believe that faith worked both ways. I thought that no matter what I had faith in, even if it wasn't the will of God, it would work. Letting go has taught me that it was okay to stop carrying the burdens of others; the only person I have control over is myself. Letting go was the strongest thing that I had to do. I had to learn to walk away, believing that what God had for me wouldn't pass me by if I stayed aligned with Him.

Allowing Myself to Heal

I collected pain and carried it for years. At some point, I lost myself; the real me was hidden underneath pain. I held onto hurtful words that people spoke over me. I allowed the disappointments that happened when my life turned left to ruin the expectations of my life going forward. I carried the heaviness that accompanied feelings of inadequacy, low self-esteem, and loneliness, and I lost my sense of purpose. Healing takes time. It doesn't happen overnight and for some, it may take longer. There are many layers to healing. I found that sharing my journey helped shed light on things that were difficult for me to see. Healing takes courage. An important contribution to my healing is figuring out how to forgive myself and how to move on from painful situations.

I believe that in order to find healing you have to first identify and acknowledge the areas where you are hurting. If you don't know how to identify what is going on it will be hard to call it out.

It is absolutely ok to say I need help. There is nothing shameful in wanting to become better. We focus so much on hiding because we are ashamed to be judged and ridiculed. There were times when I didn't allow myself to heal because

I allowed the voice of society to push me back into an area that I needed to heal from.

I shared a message about losing my job and the constant movement in the automotive industry. What I didn't share is how broken I was chasing after a career.

I didn't allow myself to heal from things that were causing me strife. There were so many things that went on during those years. I realized I didn't heal from it, I swept it under the rug. One of my old managers once told me I was smart enough to find another job, like what I went through wasn't an issue. I was even told that I should have no problem finding another job because the unemployment rate is at an absolute low.

The world can try and dictate what's next for you if you allow them to. What I discovered after losing my job and not knowing where to start over or how I would do it is that mental health is important. And while the others were screaming that the unemployment rate is low, I was screaming that the mental health rate was on a climb because people like myself needed help. I went on job interviews and did phone interviews and all I heard was what they needed from me. And what I needed was healing. I needed someone to listen to what I went through and what it cost me. I needed an outlet.

I saw myself going into a dark place, but I couldn't allow anyone to have that type of hold over me. I worked out five days a week to sort through my feelings to clear my mind. I walked twenty and sometimes thirty miles a week and I lifted weights. Life was closing in on me. I prayed daily and I found God in my situation. I knew if I didn't control my situation, it would control me.

Taking time for myself and healing was necessary for me. I needed to grab hold of the root of my feelings. What was really affecting me. So many things had happened to me over the years and this was the final straw that broke me. I made a promise to myself that I would not go into my future carrying the baggage of my past.

So many people struggle because they haven't found healing or don't know how to heal. I found healing in fighting for my truth, I stood up for myself by addressing my feelings about being let go. It's absolutely not ok to be treated unfairly.

I found healing by taking control over my situation. I have a voice, so I utilized it. Sometimes a whistle has to be blown to draw attention to something and to say it is not ok. I was determined to be heard. I found healing when I decided to redirect my life and speak out for others that have endured what I've been through but are afraid to speak up and speak out against it. I could have stayed in that place of brokenness, anger, and shame but what good would have come from it.

Through my writing, I found an outlet. Being able to share my story, my pain, and progression, has been healing. Exercising and counseling were detrimental to my healing process as well. Find your opening that will allow you to detoxify yourself from the things that attempt to hold you back. Don't allow negative situations to have a permanent impact on you. Rid yourself from the things that can possibly hold you back from experiencing your best life.

Being Whole

finally reached a point where I didn't look to someone else to validate me. I accepted me for who I am. I no longer needed someone else to love me in order to feel loved because I am loved. I love myself. I love myself enough to protect me and my peace. I started to think about all of the wonderful qualities that I have and reminded myself why I am more than enough. I'm smart, I'm intelligent, I'm successful, I'm charming, and I'm funny. My list goes on and on. I didn't need anyone else to see my qualities. I know that they exist. My journey to wholeness started by me recognizing what caused those damaged ends to grow. I was honest with myself and acknowledged what I was fighting. I reminded myself daily that I chose to be healed. I stopped blaming others for my pain or setbacks; I was no longer going to be a victim. I forgave the people who I was blaming. Finally, every day, I asked God for healing. Know that it is ok to forgive yourself for going through it and for so long. Forgiveness is freeing and definitely a part of being whole. I made up this joke between God and me.

"God," I would ask, "does heaven have a clock?"

"Why are you asking?" God would respond.

"Because I'm always late!" I laughed.

"People are always looking at me crazy because I'm never on time. I'm trying to live like my prayer, that Your will be done on earth as it is in heaven. If there is no time frame in heaven, let there be no time frame on earth."

Spending Time Alone

I think it's good for a person to spend time alone. It will allow you a chance to discover who you are. The best part about being alone is not having to answer to anyone. A part of enjoying yourself is learning how to be alone without being lonely. I enjoy my time alone because it allows me to think clearly without being bothered. Being alone allows me to be still and in my stillness. I can hear from God. I used to be afraid that I would never find love and end up alone. I thought that being alone was the worst thing ever. I finally realized that it's not. The worst thing would be, having someone and still being alone. I reached a place in life where I could embrace my singleness. I needed quiet time to examine my life openly and honestly. There is absolutely no rush. I needed to take a break from everyone and spend time alone to experience, appreciate, and love myself.

As I continue to grow and sort through life, I've found that this time alone has been necessary. Some of my most powerful memories have been openly sharing my struggles and the healing that came from going to the altar for prayer. I started acknowledging the things that have caused me to be broken so that I could address it and heal properly.

Alone time allows an opportunity to focus on myself and give myself everything that I need to get better. Being alone can help build mental strength. For years, I spent a lot of time working and volunteering. I benefit from spending some alone time. I spent so much time working and helping others, I never stopped to think about how to get the most out of my life. I was constantly giving myself to someone or something.

I was always too busy to make some time for myself. What I found to be true while being alone is that being alone with my thoughts gave my mind a chance to wonder which has helped me to become more creative. I was attuned with my thoughts. This helped me figure out what was next for me on my journey to finding purpose.

Spending time alone gave me a chance to ensure there is a purpose for everything that I've endured. A nice quiet space provided an opportunity for me to think about my story, how I wanted to express it, and what I wanted to see manifest from it. It changed my outlook on how I wanted to share what I've been going through.

I've become comfortable in my own skin and I've been able to make choices without a spare of influence and that helped me to develop insight into who I am as a person. Creating quiet time for myself allowed me to become the best version of myself

Finding Out Who I Am

I know who I am, but I'm not the person I was. No one else's approval is needed. Knowing who you are is the greatest wisdom a person can have. What are your goals? What are your needs? What are the things you value? As we continue to grow older, those things may change, and you may look at life differently. When we surround ourselves with diverse people and our experiences change, life appears to us differently and we evolve. Always, love yourself for who you are and not who someone wants you to be.

Stand strong on who you are and don't let anyone define you. What I have learned is people will keep their past behind them but place your past in front of them. It's okay for them to change and be forgiven but be a constant reminder of who you used to be.

My gifts allowed me to see the person that I am. The more I walk in purpose the more developed I become, and I can see my character. Knowing who I am is the beginning of wisdom. It is the most important skill I could ever possess.

When I really began to know myself, I realized what I needed to do. I didn't look for others to validate me or give me permission to move forward in becoming. I was confident in my decisions.

Knowing myself allowed me to go around the annoyance of wasting time in the wrong things. I've had my shares of ups and down which has helped me to grow. The confidence that I gained helped me to understand my purpose and I began to make bigger impacts on the world. I no longer wanted to live for me, I wanted to make a difference and sow into generations behind me. I want to help make them better.

Finding out your true identity unlocks your purpose. Once you find your purpose you become relentless and unstoppable.

Spend Time with God

My life has always been busy, and I thought that I was doing something by pretending to be an energizer bunny. I didn't make time for God like I should have. I spent very little time with Him.

It was in my season of sorting through my life and properly healing is when I started to spend time with God. It was the only way I would be able to know who I am. No one knows me better than my creator. I went straight to the source for answers and restoration.

Spending time with God was daily conversation with Him. It was stillness. It was long talks while showering. Constant questions of what is next. And even singing praises and worship while I was driving to and from work. There is no right or wrong way to spend time with God. There is no right or wrong way to have a conversation with Him.

I can recall texting God like a friend. I texted my friends when I wanted to talk. One day, I decided to text God and have a full conversation with Him. I created a number for God and decided to text him daily. This was the best idea I have ever come up with. Every time I got the urge to talk to my friend, I would text 432826, which stands for heaven and I saved it in my phone as God. If I can become creative with everything else, I could become creative with my relationship with God. I even emailed myself and sent letters to God. It's all about communication. It takes effort to find the time and energy to connect with God on a regular basis. These were things I did every day, so it was only right that I do it for Him. I was still getting to Him like I needed to.

God has given me the ability to create innovative ideas, so I've decided to use that talent to pursue Him.

If he used His resources (people, miracles, signs, and wonders) to get to me it is only right that I use what I have to get to Him. Psalm 150:6 says, let everything that has breath praise the Lord. The Bible doesn't say, "Let everyone who has time praise the Lord." However you choose to spend time with God is up to you so do something that creates a special bond.

Pursue Purpose

I don't think a day goes by without me wondering about my purpose. What is the reason for which I exist? Why was I created? I was beating myself up and worrying; leaving a legacy and living with purpose is important to me. I had to learn to appreciate where I am in my journey, even if I'm not where I want to be. Every season in my life serves a purpose. As I pursued purpose, I never became complacent. I never allowed myself to get comfortable. I sought challenges. I continued to push myself to become better. And no matter what people thought of me, even when they tried to break me, I allowed God to strengthen me, so that I could continue to move forward.

My life changed the day I said yes to myself and took back control. The movement began when I snatched up fear and tossed it out of the window. No longer would I believe that my current mental state was all God had for me. I would've never imagined that breaking up with someone or losing my job would take me on an expedition of healing my heart. In order to do that, I had to do some soul searching. The procedure was not by accident; it was an act of fate.

The first thing I learned was self-care. Self-care is more than just pampering yourself. You have to take good care of yourself. Good self -care goes beyond getting your nails done, hair done, and taking yourself on a date. These things are vital; you want to be able to treat yourself and not wait on anyone else. My outer appearance is significant, but my inner person was just as important. I was perfecting my outer appearance, yet neglecting my mind, body, and soul. No one would ever know what I was hiding internally. I masked it underneath my beauty because that is what people do. I would buy designer clothes and shoes, expensive bags, and apply my MAC cosmetics, but it's all to create a façade. My flawless public facade masked private despair.

The second thing I learned was self-love. My best practice of self-love was when I stopped doing things to make other people happy. I went above and beyond for people that could care less. When I realized that I was being taken advantage of, I decided to put myself first with no remorse. I set boundaries and stayed within. I learned to become married to my happiness and well-being. The practice of self-love is associated with a multitude of benefits, such as greater life satisfaction, increased happiness, and greater resilience.

The third thing I learned was how to heal. I started healing when I decided to let go of my past, let go of the pain, hurt, guilt, and grudges for things I had no control over. I figured out that letting go of things that jeopardized my peace or sanity was imperative. Once I started to heal under the surface, I placed value on who I am. I had to go as far back as my upgrowing. There was pain from my childhood that spilled over into my adulthood that needed to be captured. No longer could I allow that pain to be in control of me. Finding healing has been a liberating experience.

One year, I attended a retreat called Healing the Heart and that experience led me to dig deeper. I was so focused on my current situation that I didn't realize the real issues were underlining what was on the surface. It was like a doctor had said, "the problem isn't the heart attack; it's the clogged arteries that led to the heart attack." My issues didn't stem from the breakup my failed relationships had had. It was the people I allowed into my life and once I began to observe others, I could reflect on it. There had been pain I had carried for years that led me into that bad relationship. It was time to clean up the mess and call it what it was.

The last thing I learned was how to find purpose. When I started my weight loss journey, I wanted to lose weight and build confidence. Somewhere along the journey, I discovered self-esteem, power, and reassurance. I began to believe in myself and started seeing dreams that I had prayed for years ago come to fruition. As I shed the weight, I began to stretch towards my destiny. I started envisioning my goals and reaching towards Heaven to release them. The journey of life can be more than we imagine if we are open enough to welcome it.

As you continue to take your life to another level, take time to dissect the weeded areas that are causing you pain or holding you back from a purposeful life. Often, we think our past stays in the past as it should, but don't let your past hold you back from creating your greatest future. Some things need to be addressed and dealt with. Pain can only disguise itself and stay hidden for so long. Eventually, it will revisit your life and you will have to unmask the things you've kept hidden.

There were many bumps in the road for me. If I allowed all the times, I couldn't pay bills or run out of money to dictate what my future would look like, I would still be in that cycle of not being able to take care of myself. Deep down, I knew there was more for me. I knew that God had an even greater plan. There is purpose in me. I just had to want to find out what it was and how to get it to manifest.

This went beyond having more money because a better paying job doesn't mean you have purpose. I had chased money for years and was miserable. I wanted more for myself. I wanted the six-figure income and a title, but it cost me my health and mental space to get it. Dr. Myles Munroe once said, "Don't ever chase money (or anything) because it will run from you."

I've reached a point in my life where I don't aspire to be successful; I aspire to make a difference. Finally, I found purpose and it was from changing my mindset. Once I changed the way I thought, I changed the way I lived. It is my hope that you can use this book and my life's examples to push into your purpose and be a shining light to the future of someone else.

There is a saying that our best days are ahead of us. If the days ahead of us are better than the days behind us how does that happen? How can I make that happen when I wake up each day believing things will get better and some days it was worse? As I pondered on this for a while, I started to realize there was more to the saying.

Everything in the earth goes in full circulation. What I do affects the next generation. That means the days ahead of them will be better because of the changes that I've prepared for them. It is our purpose to set them up for greatness. We have to teach them to sow back into the earth so that it could circulate for what's behind them.

Even though everyday doesn't appear to be better it is because my life is certainly better than the person who went before me and we must continue to make things better for the next generation.

As you push yourself into purpose think about everyone that is coming behind you and think about what you want to leave for them. Think about a situation that you had to go through and as you walk through it be sure to leave a positive impact. Some battles we fight or fought are so that the next generation doesn't have to endure it.